EVERYDAY SISU

EVERYDAY
SISU

Tapping into Finnish
Fortitude for a Happier,
More Resilient Life

Katja Pantzar

A TARCHERPERIGEE BOOK

An imprint of Penguin Random House LLC
penguinrandomhouse.com

Most TarcherPerigee books are available at special quantity discounts for bulk purchase for sales promotions, premiums, fund-raising, and educational needs. Special books or book excerpts also can be created to fit specific needs. For details, write: SpecialMarkets@penguinrandomhouse.com.

Hardcover ISBN: 9780593419267
eBook ISBN: 9780593419274

Printed in the United States of America
10   9   8   7   6   5   4   3   2   1

While the author has made every effort to provide accurate information at the time of publication, neither the publisher nor the author assumes any responsibility for errors or changes that occur after publication.

Neither the publisher nor the author assumes any responsibility for third-party websites or their content.

Further, neither the publisher nor the author is engaged in rendering professional advice or services to the individual reader. The ideas presented in this book are not intended as a substitute for consulting with your physician. All matters regarding your health require medical supervision. Neither the author nor the publisher shall be liable or responsible for any loss or damage allegedly arising from any information or suggestion in this book.

Author's note: This is my personal story. I am not a medical expert, scientist, therapist, personal trainer, or nutritionist. The ideas presented here are founded on fact-based interviews, information, and research on Finnish ways to better care for our mental and physical well-being, as well as one another and the planet.

For Felix

CONTENTS

EVERYDAY SISU

PROLOGUE

ON AN OVERCAST day in February, I'm riding my bicycle through the streets of Helsinki toward a wellspring of culture and well-being housed in a grand neoclassical 1841 building by the sea.

It's cold, and as I feel a blustery, bone-chilling wind that's familiar from living in rainy cities such as Vancouver on Canada's west coast, where I grew up, I start to pedal faster in an effort to warm up.

I pass a young couple bundled up in their winter coats, wearing colorful scarves and hats. Walking together, they are holding hands, which makes me smile and gives me a sense of hope about the future.

As I cycle off the pavement onto a gravel road that leads into the parklike setting housing the complex, my destination is Visit Peace, a new wellness space that's tucked into Lapinlahden Lähde (*lähde* means "spring" in Finnish), a community center that focuses on arts and culture and mental and physical well-being in a range of ways that incorporate the role of nature.

Although I'm heading to do an interview with the founder of Visit Peace for a magazine article, I must confess that I've already fallen in love with the center's name, for who wouldn't like to visit peace? So many people around the world seem to be struggling with the stresses and demands of modern life on so many levels.

On a personal level, as someone who suffers from depression and anxiety from time to time and has a tendency to take on too much and then crash because my energy is depleted, I feel I could benefit from practical help in better understanding how to manage my own mental and physical energy, as well as bigger-picture societal issues such as the state of the planet.

Since moving from North America to Finland many years ago, I've become fascinated by sisu, the unique Finnish concept of resilience, courage, and grit in the face of all manner of challenges. Through ongoing research, I'm convinced that a good sense of sisu holds the key to helping us all develop a greater sense of resilience in dealing with the challenges we face daily, whether big or small.

A few years ago, I wrote a book about Finnish well-being, sharing the story of how I had gradually adopted many elements of the Nordic lifestyle after moving to Finland. I spoke about how I gained strength and better mental and physical health by embracing simple and sensible activities such as spending more time outdoors in nature with friends no matter what the weather, and taking up popular activities such as winter swimming and year-round cycling.

I interviewed a range of experts and regular folk to ensure factual and science-based information was included on the various topics, such as the health benefits of the Finnish sauna steam bath. *The Finnish Way* was translated into twenty-two languages and published in twenty-two countries (thanks to my agent), and since then I've received a fairly steady stream of interview requests from around the world from media ranging from NBC to *El País*. This media interest has been fueled in part by the fact that Finland has been named the world's happiest country for four years in a row (2018 to 2021) by the *World Happiness Report*, a publication of the UN Sustainable Development Solutions Network, which uses a range of metrics to rank the quality of people's lives.

At around the same time, I was juggling my work as a free-lance writer, editor, and journalist along with major life changes such as the end of a long-term relationship, which left me doing a lot of solo parenting (I have an absolutely amazing eleven-year-old son) and reevaluating many aspects of my life. Even with a very supportive family and a close network of friends, I started to seriously falter.

And then my own sense of sisu took a significant tumble.

Overwhelmed by all of life's demands, I began having a hard time keeping up. I also made the fatal mistake of not heeding my own sisu advice, which in a nutshell is to practice simple self-care so that you can take care of others. Scrambling to manage everything, I was spending less time in nature, in the water, on my bicycle, and not doing commonsense things such as eating and resting properly.

I felt exhausted and depleted much of the time, and my general sense of malaise was also seeping into other areas of my life, disturbing my sleep. I would often wake up in the middle of the night in a panic, worried about work, finances, and relationships.

At times, it felt as though everyone wanted a piece of me, and in my earnestness to respond, I sometimes gave toxic people and situations—both in my personal and professional life—too much of my limited energy.

At some point I also started to suffer from impostor syndrome for having written a book about well-being that so many people around the world interpreted as a guide to happiness.

The title of that first book in several territories, including the United States, featured the word *happiness* in the subtitle. As such, I was often asked in media interviews to be a spokesperson for how to achieve that seemingly elusive goal, especially because of Finland's designation as the world's happiest country in the *World Happiness Report.*

While the report's metrics for happiness are based on well-being indicators such as good social support networks, trust, honest governments, safe environments, and healthy lives, and a strong part of my message was about creating joy and resilience by tackling life's daily challenges through lifestyle choices, I felt uncomfortable in this new role as a happiness ambassador. Open about my own lifelong struggles with depression and anxiety, I had underlined the fact that I wasn't—by any stretch—miraculously cured. Rather, I wanted to share with others the practical ways to manage malaise and improve physical and mental well-being that I had discovered.

At the same time, I was receiving messages on social media from readers around the world thanking me for my work and inspiration.

Yet I felt like I was sinking. And struggling to surface.

Then the coronavirus pandemic hit in spring 2020, dramatically impacting the daily lives of billions of people around the world on so many levels. Like so very many others, I was overwhelmed by what was happening, and I tried to make sense of it all and stay upbeat. Truth be told, I felt a sense of impending doom. Add to that the stress of trying to do the right things to stay safe, adapting to suddenly being very socially isolated with my son, whose school temporarily closed, and working from home, while worrying about the health and well-being of my friends and family, including my parents, who live 4,663 miles (as the crow flies) away on Canada's west coast.

After a long stretch of pushing too hard and too fast, I completely burned out in the summer of 2020.

As I know now, in the lead-up to complete exhaustion—the kind in which simple tasks such as brushing your teeth can seem insurmountable and pointless—many people think that if they try harder to do more, they'll feel better and push through.

Which is exactly what I did. But it made everything so much worse. Still in recovery mode from dealing with previous traumas, I was already weak on the ground when the pandemic hit. Yet somehow, in my growing state of mental and physical exhaustion, I rationalized that stopping would lead me to collapse. But if I kept going, I would regain my sense of strength, my sense of sisu.

There are sayings in many languages and cultures that hold a similar truth: Sometimes you need to hit rock bottom before you can grow and rebuild.

That's what happened to me.

After being hospitalized for serious clinical depression (that was the official diagnosis, caused in part by total burnout), I began the slow and often challenging process of recovery, of rebuilding my sense of sisu, or fortitude, in old and new ways, as I was forced to accept that my previous methods of attempting to function were no longer feasible.

As I learned to walk again—quite literally, for at my lowest, weakest point I was nearly bedridden—I started to explore the idea of sisu from different angles, such as that of good healthy daily sisu, which meant learning to manage my energy and resources in a new way. This included learning seemingly obvious yet new-to-me skills such as saying no when necessary, as I have a tendency to say yes out of a sense of polite obligation and because I often get overly excited about many things at once and want to do them all. I have also tended to be a people pleaser, even at my own expense.

Like so many women, I was raised at a time in North

America when women were taught to put their own needs and dreams after those of others, especially men.

There's a common stereotype about the polite Canadian who apologizes when somebody else bumps into them. Though it may be a cliché, it holds a deeper symbolism: being overly polite and nice is about saying sorry even when someone else does something potentially hurtful to you. And as nice as it may seem, that can be a problem.

While it goes without saying that we all need to deal with difficult people at times and can't just left-swipe them away, we can, however, learn how to deal with those who make us feel uneasy, whether they are simply rude, toxic, or actual bullies, through good, healthy, peaceful sisu.

As an empath, it has taken me a lifetime to learn how to effectively deal with emotionally abusive people by setting firm yet diplomatic boundaries. I also had to acknowledge that part of the reason I felt so poorly was because I had let some of those people metaphorically walk all over me. So long as you allow certain behaviors to continue, you are facilitating them.

This was among the important lessons I learned, along with the idea that good sisu also means having the courage to ask for help when you need it, instead of trying to take care of and manage everything on your own.

I also had to learn simple lessons such as if I didn't get

everything on my to-do list done this minute, this hour, or this day, that was all right. It didn't mean I was a failure, a bad person, or lazy. The rest of the list would still be there later. This was a difficult transition for a recovering, overly self-critical multi-multitasker who was often willing to lend a hand or do something for someone else even when it meant going out of my way.

As part of my recovery, it was imperative that I gently return to self-care, by taking baby steps such as going for a short walk or a dip in the sea. These may sound like simple activities, but because I had spent several months physically inactive, my overall physical fitness was extremely poor.

Embarking on a journey to redevelop a healthy sense of sisu, I also sharpened my focus on how I could offer my son the best tools for his future. I became more concerned about the state of the natural world and started to pay more attention to finding positive ways to effect change and include more sustainability actions in our daily lives.

As I've long supported solutions and constructive journalism—that is, looking for real-world solutions and positive stories of ways to tackle humanity's many challenges—I kept coming across signs of hope, of ways to solve the problems big and small facing us all.

Some were concrete examples, such as the successful

Finnish model for addressing the problem of homelessness in Helsinki, or the news story that popped up in my feed about a Finnish company making protein out of thin air to disconnect food production from agriculture in an effort to address two huge challenges: climate change and world hunger.

Other signs of hope were words, thoughts, and ideas that gave me positive pause for thought.

Although this is not intended as a political book, it must be said that the political infrastructure of where you live directly impacts the quality of your life. For example, whether or not you live in a country with universal medical care has a massive impact on your mental and physical health and that of your neighbors.

As I looked around for inspiration, I came across it in unlikely places.

"The strength of a society is measured not by the wealth of its most affluent members, but by how well its most vulnerable citizens are able to cope," said Finnish prime minister Sanna Marin in her New Year 2020 address. Though as a journalist I have a healthy skepticism regarding what politicians say, I believe Marin's words address a central principle of the Finnish social system, in that it aims to provide support (and sisu) for all its citizens.

Marin, who at thirty-five is one of the world's youngest

heads of state, grew up in a rainbow family. Her message, which is in such sharp contrast to the views of some other world leaders, including those who are dead set against helping those less fortunate or accepting those who identify with something other than the perceived mainstream, resonates on many levels and offers hope.

As I've embraced a new set of Nordic values to replace some of the consumerist ones that I grew up with, I've also realized how important it is to take care of ourselves, one another, and Mother Earth.

And it seems to me that Lapinlahden Lähde provides an excellent starting point, as it's the source of a number of groundbreaking firsts.

The center is housed in what was once Finland's first specialized psychiatric hospital—it's where playwright and writer Aleksis Kivi (1834–1872), who wrote the first significant novel in Finnish, *Seven Brothers*, spent time being treated for chronic melancholy, which is better known today as depression.

Kivi provides a concrete example of Marin's idea of helping society's most vulnerable, which is part of the Finnish ideal of giving everyone an equal and fair chance, regardless of his or her background. Case in point, Kivi grew up in rural poverty but went on to study at the University of Helsinki and became a lauded playwright and writer.

The Lapinlahden Lähde center also speaks to the power of working together to address many of the issues that face us all. It's home to Restaurant Loop, Finland's first waste-food restaurant, which serves ingredients, donated by local grocery stores, that are close to their expiration date but still perfectly edible, in an effort to address climate change (food waste is one of the leading contributors).

On the grounds near the waterfront is Helsinki's reportedly oldest public sauna, that quintessential Finnish cultural icon lauded for its numerous health benefits. There's also an on-site urban nature center and cafés, as well as an upcycling plant exchange, a few thrift shops, and several venues that offer services from physical and mental therapy to exercise classes in nature and cultural activities.

As I search for answers, I know that I am not alone in my quest. I continually meet people who have experienced great challenges and traumas and tapped into their own forms of sisu and recovered, rebounded, and rebuilt their lives in new ways. I admire those who share their stories and vulnerabilities and provide inspiration for others, because I firmly believe that we all struggle and the only way forward is to help one another.

If there's a sentence that sums up my quest, it's the title of Canadian writer Sheila Heti's experimental novel, *How Should a Person Be?* For it's a question that I so often ask myself. Am I doing the right things for the world? To help others? To try to make a positive impact?

In my quest I start to develop a type of daily sisu, which means looking for simple ways that anyone can take easy, practical steps to improve their mental and physical resilience in dealing with the challenges of everyday life. And along the way I have found so many pivotal answers of everyday fortitude from a range of experts as well as so many wise, good-hearted humans.

For in taking care of ourselves and our collective sisu lies the key to helping others and the world.

We are all in this together.

CHAPTER 1

SISU EVERY DAY

Finding Fortitude During Tough Times

ON A CRISP autumn morning I stood on a wooden dock that juts out into the Baltic Sea in central Helsinki. Wearing only my bathing suit, I placed my towel and change of clothes onto one of the wooden tables as I chatted with my fellow cold-water swimmers about the weather, the water temperature (it's a brisk 9 degrees Celsius, 48.2 degrees Fahrenheit), and the state of world affairs during the coronavirus pandemic, which has dramatically changed the lives of so many people around the globe.

This day's dip into the sea was really just a dip, as I'm not a very good swimmer. But this simple morning routine has become one of the activities that make up part of my lifeline.

The fact that I was able to get myself to the dock, an easy five-minute walk from home, go for a dip, and talk with friends is little short of a miracle, or at least a 180-degree turnaround. For less than two months earlier, I was in a very different place—I was recovering from a serious depressive episode of burnout that left me so depleted that the mere idea of this morning's activities would have seemed impossible.

Yet here I was, basking in the rays of sunshine that seem like a precious commodity as we head toward the dark months of winter, when there will be only a few hours of daylight here in the Nordics.

After my dip I walked over to the bushes lining the shores of the island where I live with my son, to pick a few wild sea buckthorns. The small tangerine-colored berries are also known as liquid gold, as they are rich in vitamins C and E, fiber, and essential fatty acids. A handful of sea buckthorns is said to boast the same amount of vitamin C as a medium-size orange.

Because of a concept called everyman's right (*jokamiehen oikeus*), or public access rights, everyone in Finland is allowed to enjoy outdoor pursuits from forests to lakes and the sea and activities such as picking wild berries, mushrooms, and flowers so long as you don't disturb other people or their property, or damage the environment.

Then I walked the short distance home along the gravel

path past the docked off-duty icebreakers, up the small hill, and through the picturesque yard of my son's school, which comprises a collection of buildings, some of which date back to the 1840s, including an Instagrammable brick façade.

Once home, after a hot shower, I had a cup of strong black coffee that tasted even better after my bracing but invigorating mini-swim.

A few months ago, I was so anxious that the mere suggestion of a short walk to the dock was overwhelming. I couldn't drink anything other than decaf coffee for fear that I would start shaking. So what happened and why is cold-water swimming one of the keys to my recovery? How does it build fortitude and sisu?

Building Resilience

While there has been research into the positive physiological effects of cold-water swimming, the idea of cross-adaptation is a slightly newer area of focus.

Essentially, cross-adaptation means that adapting to one stressor can help you adapt to others. This concept is one of the key discoveries I made that set me on a journey to uncovering how people train their resilience or sisu skills so that they have the ability to adapt, survive, and even thrive in the face of great challenges such as major life changes or loss.

So while this cool habit of mine quite literally shocks me into feeling better both mentally and physically, as it triggers the so-called happy hormones (which include endorphins, the body's natural painkillers; serotonin; dopamine; and oxytocin), it also helps me to deal with other stresses in my life.

With the cold-water swimming boom that's sweeping parts of Europe and North America, especially following the time when the coronavirus pandemic shuttered swimming pools and had people looking for safer exercise alternatives, there's actually some science behind the hobby.

In a 2020 *BBC Science Focus* article titled "Cold Water Swimming: Why an Icy Dip Is Good for Your Mental and Physical Health," writer Helen Glenny interviews Professor Mike Tipton, an environmental physiologist at the University of Portsmouth in the UK and a leading cold-water swimming researcher.

According to Tipton, after the initial cold-water shock response, adaptation happens over the longer term. This type of adaptation makes people less reactive to the shock of the cold water, but could also make them less reactive to stress, he tells the BBC.

This concept of cross-adaptation forms one piece of the puzzle that I've been looking to solve. When it comes to the idea of sisu, that unique brand of strength in the face of challenges, so many people I've met who have survived great setbacks and gone on to flourish tell me that some sort of cross-adaptation (though they don't call it by that name) has been instrumental in their pivot. This holds true whether the trauma they've recovered from is a serious illness, a physically or mentally abusive relationship, an accident, or the loss of a loved one or a job.

And they all seem to share a similar motto, which is: "It's okay not to be okay."

"It's okay not to be okay."

To use the old cliché, when life hands you lemons, some people make lemonade. I'm on a mission to find out how and why, in hopes that it can truly help us all.

Positive, healthy sisu doesn't come from what you can do, it comes from overcoming what you thought you couldn't.

• • •

IT'S FAIR TO say that 2020 gave just about everyone in the world a simultaneous sucker punch. With the onset of the coronavirus pandemic, so many people faced health concerns and work and financial worries as the world felt the impact of

COVID-19. Social distancing and remote working introduced a new set of obstacles that in turn led to an increase in loneliness, depression, and anxiety.

Challenges in maintaining overall health grew as gyms and pools were closed in an effort to curb the spread of the virus.

Mental and physical well-being are inextricably linked.

Pre-pandemic, the statistics were already alarming: one billion people lived with a mental health issue, according to the World Health Organization (WHO). And for anyone who is skeptical about the extent of the global mental health crisis, here's a chilling statistic from the WHO: even before the coronavirus pandemic, in 2019, the second leading cause of death among young people (fifteen to twenty-nine years of age) around the world was suicide.

· · ·

DURING THE ONSET of the global COVID-19 crisis in spring 2020, venerable fashion bible *Vogue* featured a profile of Finnish prime minister Sanna Marin.

In the well-researched piece, *Vogue* writer Sirin Kale cites that special quality of Finnish fortitude as part of the key to understanding Marin's modus operandi. According to Kale, sisu, that unique form of stoicism, determination, resilience, and can-do attitude, describes both the Finnish national character and Marin; the author likens it to both taking a bracing dip in a freezing sea and gritting your teeth while shaking hands with your political enemies.

Marin took the country's top position in December 2019 when former prime minister Antti Rinne was forced to resign following controversy surrounding his handling of a series of postal strikes.

Marin, who has been active in politics from a young age, previously held the post of minister of transportation and communication before stepping into the PM position. For many, she represents the Finnish dream of equal opportunity on several levels, including the fact that she grew up in a rainbow family at a time when it was not yet widely accepted, let alone talked about. After her mother and father split up when she was very young, her mother and her mother's female partner raised her.

One of Marin's main messages, whether delivered at home or abroad, has been that the goal of her five-party coalition government is to build a society that is socially, environmentally, and economically sustainable. This message is one of the core elements of sisu. The only viable way forward is to care not only for one another but also for society's most vulnerable, and for the natural world.

In many interviews and speeches, including one that Marin delivered at the UN's International Women's Day event in New York City in March 2020 (before the coronavirus lockdown), Marin has repeatedly stressed the fact that she wants to ensure that everyone has the building blocks for a good life, no matter what their background or gender.

In my quest to better understand the Finnish quality of sisu, everyday courage or resilience in the face of great challenges, I'm drawn to the stories of people who face great obstacles—as we all do at various points in our lives—and turn them around to work to their advantage instead of being overwhelmed or giving up.

Whether it's emotional or physical resilience, what are the tools required? Where do people find the strength, the sisu, to deal with smaller, daily setbacks and bigger ones such as serious illness or a devastating accident? And how is it that some people manage to turn vulnerabilities and setbacks around and pivot into strength, growth, or even a new path in life? How can sisu be used to combat fear or things that are out of your personal control? What does it take to start a new career later in life? Why is it important to stand up for what you believe in and support others? How can you use peaceful sisu to deal with difficult people and bullies? That's what I want to find out.

Meet the Goddess of Sisu

The best place to start, of course, is with the world's first academic sisu researcher, Emilia Elisabet Lahti, whose current focus is on sisu as a gentle superpower.

When I first met Lahti in 2017 for research on my first book, I was immediately struck by the fact that she's one of those rare people whose inner light shines brightly and warmly outward. Along the way, she has become a friend, a confidante, and a sister in sisu.

As a trailblazer, Lahti honed her research at the University of Pennsylvania under the guidance of psychology greats such as American professors Angela Duckworth, author of *New York Times* bestseller *Grit: The Power of Passion and Perseverance*; and Martin Seligman, widely considered to be one of the pioneers of positive psychology. Quite simply, Lahti, who overcame domestic abuse to become an ultrarunner and academic (among her many other achievements), is a sisu goddess.

When Lahti's first research article, "Embodied Fortitude: An Introduction to the Finnish Construct of *Sisu*," was published in the *International Journal of Wellbeing* in 2019, it went on to be awarded best article of the year by the journal.

In addition to being a doctoral candidate at Finland's prestigious Aalto University School of Science, Lahti is a keynote speaker and human rights activist. Her academic work provides possibly the world's first peer-reviewed sisu study, examining the concept of Finnish fortitude and placing it in a modern-day context. She is a forerunner bringing sisu into the twenty-first century.

Many of the historic examples of sisu, a cultural concept that dates back more than five hundred years, reference great achievements and victories in war and sport—often by men. "The transition of sisu into a positive quality and national narrative was partially backed by the Finnish long distance running success in the late 19th and early 20th centuries. During the Winter War in 1939–1940, sisu was lifted to an elevated status because of Finland's miraculous opposition to the mammoth-size Red Army," Lahti writes in "Embodied Fortitude."

Sisu is a Finnish word that goes back hundreds of years and a quality that Finns hold dear, but the phenomenon is universal, according to Lahti.

Finland's history of overcoming great difficulties including devastating wars and economic recessions provides the backdrop for expertise in sisu, a concept that goes back to the 1500s, when it first appeared in written texts referring to both a personality trait and a quality that was part of a person's nature, the interior or inside of something, or quite literally a person's "guts."

Given its northerly location near the top of the world between the 60th and the 70th parallels and shared borders with Sweden, Norway, and Russia, Finland is also a land of light and weather extremes. During the warm summer months there's almost round-the-clock daylight that peaks in midsummer, which is in sharp contrast to the cold, dark winter months that have only a few hours of daylight at winter solstice.

Somatic Sisu of the Soul

On a dark, rainy night in February an audience of about a hundred or so women gathered to hear Lahti give a talk called "Sydämen Sisu," or "Sisu of the heart."

The evening's host was Naistenkartano, a women's non-profit organization founded in 1922 that aims to empower women and support them in achieving a positive change in their lives.

Although we didn't know it at the time, this evening would be one of the last opportunities for public gatherings of any type, as the global coronavirus pandemic would shut down virtually all forms of in-person group socializing for more than a year.

Addressing the enthusiastic crowd with a warm smile, Lahti introduced herself as a sensitive, curious world traveler who had been studying sisu for close to a decade with the goal of understanding how people overcome adversity.

As she explained it, her impetus for studying the cultural concept of Finnish fortitude was her own experiences of overcoming domestic violence in a relationship while she was living in New York in the early 2010s.

"Research is often me-search," she told the audience, who was hanging on to her every word.

"How did I survive, overcome what happened to me, and how can I help others?" she asked.

I recalled reading an interview with Lahti in a New Zealand women's weekly while she was in the island country several years before, running a series of marathons for "Sisu Not Silence," her initiative to raise awareness about interpersonal violence. In the article, Lahti referred to the self-blame and guilt that often accompany physical or mental abuse. As she told the magazine, there's a tendency for human beings to think "What is wrong with me? What am I doing wrong?" instead of realizing and acknowledging that the other person is an abuser.

A common thread that repeatedly surfaces in interviews and conversations with experts and regular folk alike is the idea that one of the keys to developing and maintaining a good sense of sisu is trying to make sense of and deal with one's own traumas and issues. This can be a powerful part of moving forward and finding meaning, which is why I felt a deep tingle when Lahti delivered the following words: "Everything that puts you down is abuse."

Abuse doesn't need to be physical; emotional abuse can be just as detrimental, which is why so many victims of bullying suffer serious long-term effects on their mental and physical well-being, including post-traumatic stress. Continual undermining leaves you doubting yourself and can make you feel awful—even long after the attacks or relationship are over.

Then Lahti delivered her next empowering line: "I will never again carry shame that never belonged to me."

For those who have been abused, it's common to carry shame and guilt, to feel responsible for what happened. If you have been repeatedly minimized, you may start to believe that that is your truth. And it can weaken you to the core.

One of the most constructive, sisu-esque things to do is to build yourself up, both mentally and physically. Do it gradually and slowly, if necessary.

This is why what Lahti said next so fully resonated: "After

abuse, corporeality, the quality of being physical, is your way to gain your power."

• • •

LAHTI'S FINDINGS, ALONG with a large body of established scientific research by other researchers, back up this mind-body theory; the somatic connection is key. She views forti-tude as "a somatic quality." In "Embodied Fortitude" she writes, "In the last few decades, an idea has been promoted in cognitive science to view the body as having a central role in shaping our mind, actions and emotions. Embodied cognition has now been fairly well established and it is the radical hy-pothesis that 'our bodies and their perceptually guided mo-tions through the world do much of the work required to achieve our goals.'"

"Embodied fortitude" is the key to maintaining balance.

Practicing what Lahti calls "embodied for-titude" is the key to maintaining balance.

Part of the key to developing a healthy sense of sisu is to take care of the physical self through movement and activities that nurture a connection to nature, as well as other strength-building exercises such as what we eat and consume, the people we spend time with, how we care for one another, and even the thoughts we think.

But where do you draw the line between what makes you stronger and finding the balance between doing enough yet not taking on too much?

A comprehensive study on sisu in well-being and working life funded by the Academy of Finland, the University of Helsinki, and VTT Technical Research Centre of Finland found that sisu is a multidimensional characteristic.

The study results, first presented in 2020, indicated that sisu fell into two categories: beneficial and harmful. Beneficial sisu enabled people to tap into their hidden strengths and move with determination toward their goals, even exceeding what they thought were their capabilities. Harmful sisu, on the other hand, could lead people to accept challenges that were too difficult and demand too much of themselves or push too hard in the wrong direction. The results also indicated that identifying an individual's various sisu-related characteristics could help improve self-awareness and personal development. This ability in turn could promote recovery and well-being at work, which helps to prevent burnout, the data illustrated.

• • •

ACCORDING TO LAHTI, sisu shares overlapping features with psychological qualities such as courage, perseverance, and grit, "but its most pronounced aspect is about tapping into previously unknown energy reserves that seem partially embodied rather than purely mental."

She writes, "We find sisu, our 'second wind' and the extent of our mental and bodily strength, not despite adversities and discomfort, but *because* of them. Akin to photosynthesis in nature, which is the complex process of transforming light energy into chemical energy, there seems to exist an equally puzzling process through which humans unearth and transform their latent energy into movement, momentum and action during moments which at first seem but dead ends."

And those stories of sisu are stories about transcending limitations across all domains of human life, from the emotional to the physical, writes Lahti. "It lends a word to the universal capacity of humans everywhere to endure in the face of adversity and take action against nearly impossible odds when needed."

Through Lahti I became acquainted with the work of William James (1842–1919), considered to be one of the fathers of modern psychology, who experienced a time of being deeply depressed and suicidal when he was in his midthirties and decided to give life one more "deliberate try." When he experienced a dark thought, he would tell himself, "I can change."

As Lahti so eloquently puts it, the Harvard professor, philosopher, physician, and prolific writer had a lifelong quest:

"What is it that keeps our lights burning and hearts hoping during the dark night of the soul, and how might we best use this knowledge to alleviate the pain of those who are currently suffering?"

Constructive Sisu

A desire to help others is universal.

Lahti says that she was drawn to positive psychology, which aims to be preventive—a few steps ahead of everything, as it were—because she wants to know what motivates people and makes them happy.

The challenge of sisu, she says, is that it's not all positive, yet it needs to be constructive, not destructive.

Her desire to know what makes people happy and what makes them tick has inspired so many other people. British author and professor Tim Lomas, a leading expert in positive psychology, credits stumbling onto Lahti's sisu research as providing the inspiration for his lexicographic project, which gathers together words and ideas from other languages and cultures that focus on well-being.

That project became the delightful 2018 book *Translating Happiness: A Cross-Cultural Lexicon of Well-Being.*

One of the ideas that Lomas explores in his book is linguistic relativism, which is the idea that language can shape thought and experience, without determining it.

He takes as one of his examples the Japanese concept of *wabi-sabi*, which means to express appreciation for ephemerality and the passage of time.

While anyone could have a sense for this particular aesthetic, a person is more likely to be aware of it in a culture that has expressly identified and defined it.

Writing in *Psychology Today*, in a piece called "What Finnish Can Teach Us About Resilience: Discovering the Secrets of Sisu," Lomas pays homage to the concept, referring to Lahti's statement on sisu as not only having the courage to take action against very slim odds but also standing up for what's right, having integrity, and taking responsibility for one's actions.

In the article, Lomas credits Lahti's ability to overcome great challenges and writes that despite her painful path, her own experience and research suggest that it was empowering, as deep reserves of sisu helped her to overcome trauma.

Those, I think, are words to live by.

CHAPTER 2

· · · · · · · · · · ·

SISU MANAGEMENT

The Benefits of Blue Therapy

WHEN IT COMES to somatic sisu—that is, physical fortitude—one of the unlikely activities I fell in love with during my time in Finland is cold-water swimming.

Quite simply, that means going for a quick icy dip in a lake, a river, or the sea—year-round, whatever the weather.

Winter swimming, also known as ice swimming, is one of the activities directly linked to Finnish happiness, as the popular pastime offers an amazing mental and physical reset and energizer that relieves stress, anxiety, depression, fatigue, and even pain. A short, thirty-second to one-minute session of nature's cryotherapy can dramatically alter how you feel physically and mentally.

For the thousands of people who practice winter swimming, which in Finland has seen a huge surge in popularity during the past few years, this pastime is an excellent example of not only simple and sensible self-care but also sisu management.

The organic activity requires little more than a bathing suit, a towel, and access to the water, which is generous throughout Finland, known as the country of thousands of lakes (there are reportedly 187,888). Helsinki, the capital city, is surrounded by eighty miles of shoreline and numerous public swimming spots that are open and accessible year-round.

As a pastime, winter or cold-water swimming represents the Nordic ideal of accessibility or equality: it's relatively inexpensive to join a public winter swimming association or club in Finland (though many now have long queues to gain membership thanks to the boom in winter swimming), or it's simply free to practice from the many public docks and swimming spots throughout the country.

Vitamin Sea

As I have a tendency to overthink, my monkey mind trying to process five hundred things at once, the shock of the cold water provides a much-needed break. It forces me to focus on the present moment, on the feeling of the waves on my shoulders, the cold weight on my arms and fingers, legs and toes. I must also concentrate on my breathing to ensure that I get back to the dock in a calm manner, which makes for a mini-meditation session in the sea. Sometimes I practice this form of breathing just to clear my chest and lungs if they're feeling congested.

After climbing out of the water, I feel energized, enjoying a swimmer's high from the rush of happy hormones that have flooded my body.

Like so many other winter swimmers, I transition from ice swimming to cold-water swimming in the spring, when the water heats up to a balmy 10 degrees Celsius (about 50 degrees Fahrenheit), because it offers such a simple, quick, and healthy reboot compared to so many of the complicated, unnatural, often expensive ways that people around the world boost their well-being.

Although there are extreme versions of cold-water immersion techniques and winter swimming practices trending internationally, for the average person (read: anyone between about the ages of nine and ninety) in Finland, the age-old practice of winter or ice swimming (*avantouinti* in Finnish), dating back to the seventeenth century, simply means going for a short dip or swim in the sea or a lake in a hole that's been carved into the ice during the snowy winter months. Many wear wool hats and neoprene slippers and gloves to keep their extremities warm.

Traditionally, this activity is followed up by a session in a hot sauna, that quintessential Finnish steam bath that relaxes body and mind and was recently added to UNESCO's Intangible Cultural Heritage of Humanity list, where it joined Indian yoga, Argentinean tango, and Beijing opera.

Cold Science

As a journalist, I follow the latest science- and fact-based research behind why an icy dip in the cold water feels so great and is so beneficial for mind and body.

In a nutshell, a dip of thirty seconds to one minute in water that's 10 degrees Celsius (50 degrees Fahrenheit) or colder sets off the happy hormones such as endorphins, serotonin, dopamine, and oxytocin.

Endorphins are the body's natural painkillers, serotonin maintains mood balance, dopamine is the neurotransmitter that helps control the brain's reward and pleasure centers and also helps to regulate movement and emotional response, while oxytocin is known as the love hormone.

As blood circulation increases and heart rate rises, post-dip there's a swimmer's high or euphoria, which is why so many winter swimmers positively beam as they emerge from the water.

• • •

IN THE AUTUMN following my spring and summer of serious burnout, one of the ways that I started rebuilding my strength was by going for very short sea dips, something that I had stopped doing for many months when my overall health deteriorated along with my motivation to do anything that required extra effort.

Fortunately, there's a dock about a two-minute walk (an absolute urban luxury) from where I live with my son in central Helsinki. During my fall of recovery, when I initially got winded just from climbing the stairs—which was shocking, as in my previously active life I'd been a year-round cyclist and open-water swimmer—I started by heading to the dock a few times a week, as my general level of fitness improved.

This was new for me, to try to go slowly and not push too fast, to start by doing a few sit-ups or push-ups rather than demanding that my body do a hundred on the spot.

This was also a lesson that I have had to keep relearning: I am not a machine and I cannot do everything all the time. Rest and recuperation are vital keys to rebuilding a sense of sisu.

A Safe Sense of Community

During the pandemic, my cold-water habit also became an important lifeline, especially when so many group activities were limited and people were starved for social contact. Not only did it provide a physical and mental pick-me-up, the wooden dock, which, like so many others that dot the country's waterfronts, was initially built for washing rag rugs laid out on wooden tables and scrubbed with pine soap before being doused with buckets of rinsing water, also offered a safe socially distanced environment.

We stood several feet apart outdoors and exchanged a few words with our fellow swimmers about the weather, the water— how cold, how clean, still, or rocky with waves it was—and the news of the day. Especially during a time of limited social contact, these moments were priceless.

Over the years, some swimmers have become good friends, and we see one another socially for a dinner party, coffee, or a walk. And there are those whom I know only by sight, not even a first name. But it doesn't matter—here we are all equal, as we've come to share our love of the restorative powers of the sea.

During difficult times, cold-water swimming is an almost certain mood-boosting exercise, as the other swimmers are— about 99 percent of the time—in an upbeat, friendly mood, owing to our happiness-inducing habit, which adds an extra element of joy and positivity to the morning.

Our habit also offered a way to start and shape the day on a positive note, to get out and do something physical before returning to a day online, working remotely from home during the pandemic.

And with the exception of those with a heart condition, it's an activity suitable for pretty much anyone. My fellow swimmers range in age from eleven to ninety, which means that I'm exposed to a range of ideas and attitudes, vital for keeping an open mind. We are not in a silo, all from the same age group or socioeconomic background. This diversity is a huge privilege, as the idea of private clubs where all the members are from the same background is stifling.

We simply share a love of the magic that the cold water performs.

One hearty winter swimmer in her seventies swims without neoprene slippers or gloves or a wool hat. In the winter, if there's fresh snow, she may even make a snow angel on the snow-covered earth on the shoreline.

There's a Finnish saying that roughly translates to "a child is healthy when they play." This is interpreted to mean kids of all ages.

• • •

OUR ACTIVITY ALSO provides a mini nature break, as one of the docks where we swim in the Baltic Sea looks out onto the water, where across the way lie several small islands, including one that's home to Helsinki's Korkeasaari Zoo. Flanking it on either side by a few miles are newer, ultramodern residential districts such as Kalasatama and Kruunuvuorenranta, with its Öljysäiliö 468, a repurposed oil silo that's been transformed into a magnificent work of light art and an event venue.

Next to our dock, the icebreakers, with delightful names such as *Sisu* and *Voima* (strength), that ply the waters during the winter months are often docked. I take inspiration from them, for *sisu* and *voima* are two of my favorite words in the Finnish language.

The act of dipping in the sea also provides a much-needed connection to nature, which soothes the soul, allowing us to go offline and take a break. A great many things that ail us in our always-on, 24-7 digital life are compounded by our lack of contact with the natural world, with the outdoors. Too many of us spend too much time going from one artificially air-conditioned or heated environment to another, in an air-conditioned or heated metal box on wheels, because the conveniences of modern life make it possible to do so.

Cold-Water Conversion

There's a lot of anecdotal evidence about the benefits of cold-water swimming, and a quick visit to one of the many local winter watering holes that dot Finland (and other Nordic countries, for that matter) should quickly dispel any doubts about the uplifting qualities of the pastime as smiling people emerge from the water.

But as a journalist and a cold-water convert, I want to know more. What's the newest fact-based science and research behind cold-water swimming? Who is studying this growing trend of self-care?

Professor Mike Tipton and his colleagues have been studying the physiological effects of cold-water immersion on the human body. While we already know about the many positive effects of a brief dip or immersion in cold water, my interest is piqued by the idea of cross-adaptation; that is, practicing one stressor—in this case cold-water immersion—to help prep the body on a cellular level for other stressors.

So how does a cold-water immersion habit increase the ability to deal with other stressors? As you adapt to the shock of the cold water, you might also become less reactive to everyday stress, Tipton told me as we connected via Zoom.

As he explains it, the process of getting into the cold water puts the body into a situation where "your blood pressure skyrockets, glucose and fats are released into your bloodstream, providing an energy source should you need to make a quick escape—the classic 'fight-or-flight' response."

Your adrenal glands release the stress hormone cortisol, while beta-endorphin hormones in the brain provide pain relief and a sense of euphoria, he explains.

Essentially, increasing psychological and behavioral resistance to the stress of the cold-water shock by building up the ability to withstand and benefit from it is training that boosts resilience to better deal with life's other stressors. Think of it as flexing the fight-or-flight response for whatever life throws your way.

"Another way to look at it is the classic 'use it or lose it,'" says Tipton, who is a cold-water swimmer himself.

The Vagus Nerve and Mental Health

Another topical area of Tipton and his team's research is the idea that cold-water swimming can stimulate the vagus nerve, which plays a key role in mental health.

Essentially, the vagus nerve (pronounced like the American city Las Vegas) is the body's longest nerve. In Latin, *vagus* means "wanderer," as the nerve actually snakes all over the body and connects the brain to organs in the body such as the gut, heart, and lungs. The tenth cranial nerve is also part of the parasympathetic nervous system, which impacts breathing, digestive function, and heart rate.

A positive feedback loop was discovered by Barbara L. Fredrickson and Bethany E. Kok at the University of North Carolina at Chapel Hill between high vagal tone and positive emotions.

In one of the research papers that Tipton sent me, he and his colleagues referred to the effectiveness of stimulating the vagus nerve with bipolar pulse generators connected to electrodes wrapped around the left vagus nerve in the neck. This procedure was approved by the US Food and Drug Administration for the treatment of drug-resistant epilepsy and depression in 1997 and 2005.

What jumps out from the abstract is the following line: "Cold immersion of the face might represent a safer and cheaper means of stimulating the vagus."

Many researchers and experts, including Tipton, advise using caution regarding face-dipping in cold water, particularly in winter. Cooling the face and head sends a signal to the sympathetic nervous system that increases the pulse. For some, this can be a contradictory message for the heart and may even lead to arrhythmia. For this reason, I've decided to put face-dipping on hold, resuming it only during the warm summer months when the Baltic Sea hovers well above 15 degrees Celsius (59 degrees Fahrenheit).

Blue Therapy

Open-water swimming offers up many other feel-good benefits, such as green and blue therapy.

While green therapy means spending time in natural areas such as parks and forests for the range of spill-off benefits on mental health, blue therapy means spending time in and near water. When it comes to cold-water and open-water swimming, there's often a sense of community, as it's an activity done with other people, and the feeling of achievement for having done something difficult.

Yes, there are mornings when the frigid temperatures, combined with driving sleet, make many a winter swimmer wonder why they've taken up such a pastime. But post-dip, the answer is clear: you feel a hundred times better.

• • •

AS MY PASSION for my pastime grows, so does my cold-water swimming community and tribe, both in real life and on social media. Members of the international open-water, cold-water winter-swimming community motivate and inspire one another, especially if someone is having a rough day and needs a little encouragement to go for a plunge.

Finland's Winter Swimmers (Suomen Avantouimarit) brings together members from throughout the country, with swimmers posting spectacular shots from Lapland, often referred to as Europe's last great wilderness, and other stunning rural and urban swimming spots throughout the country. It also inspires a kind of virtual tourism, and along with images and videos from winter swims, we share advice and useful tips.

Internationally, on social media, especially on platforms such as Instagram, there are cold-water swimmers from Norway to Germany to England to Canada whom I follow and am followed by, and we encourage and entertain one another with pictures of our cheerful wool hats and swimsuits, color-coordinated for specific holidays and occasions.

Together, we laugh at the occasional comment that follows when posting cold-water swimming pictures on social media such as "That's crazy!" To which the reply is, naturally: "Actually, this habit helps to keep me sane."

As we share the joys and challenges of winter swimming with others and inspire people around the world to try our "crazy pastime," it feels as though we're spreading some positive social media sisu.

During a difficult moment, seeing other swimmers post their post-dip-high pictures gives me the inspiration to head for the water, for no matter how grim I feel, I know in my heart that I will feel better both mentally and physically after a cold dip.

The Healing Power of Water

Connecting with nature, whether spending time in forests, parks, or near bodies of water such as the sea or lakes, and its effect on our well-being is well documented.

When it comes to blue therapy, the impressive and highly original work of Dr. Wallace J. Nichols, an American scientist, activist, community organizer, and author, comes to me through my friend and open-water swimming expert and instructor Päivi Pälvimäki.

Pälvimäki runs #wildswimmingfinland on social media, where she posts images of herself open-water swimming in magnificent places throughout Finland year-round.

One night she messaged me to highly recommend Nichols's 2014 landmark book, *Blue Mind: How Water Makes You Happier, More Connected and Better at What You Do*. According to Nichols, water is medicine for those who need it most. He writes about how chronic stress can damage the cardiovascular, immune, digestive, nervous, and musculoskeletal systems. That in turn lowers levels of dopamine and serotonin, which can make people feel exhausted and depressed.

He cites studies that have shown that stress lasting for more than twenty-one days can actually impair the function of the medial prefrontal cortex, which affects higher-level thinking, and at the same time make the amygdala—the brain's fear and aggression center—hyperactive.

This prolonged exposure to glucocorticoids, a type of steroid secreted by the adrenal glands during stress, can actually cause the cells in the hippocampus to atrophy, which is the same damage that is seen in people with PTSD, or post-traumatic stress disorder, according to Nichols.

Blue Mind illustrates how our proximity to water has a positive impact on health, creativity, and professional success as well as on our connection to the natural world and one another. After all, as Nichols aptly points out, we begin our aquatic life journey as babies in our mother's womb.

Equally vital, some 72 percent of the Earth is water, and the average adult body is 50 to 65 percent water.

In addition to the abundance of natural bodies of water in Finland, the country also boasts one of the world's highest-quality tap waters. It's pure, clean, and tasty, and you can fill your water bottle anywhere and trust that it will be safe.

Just walking along the shoreline of a beach or lake and listening to the sound of the waves or spending time beside a river can be therapeutic.

Nichols's thoughtful and fact-based writing brings me back to why water—and nature—has such a positive impact on our lives. And when we lose that connection, we also lose part of ourselves.

CHAPTER 3

GREEN THERAPY

Using Nature and Sisu for Energy Management

A CONNECTION TO NATURE is part of the sisu toolkit that can boost our well-being by helping us to deal with and reduce stress, better manage our energy levels, and find mental and physical peace.

I initially met Essi Nousu, physiotherapist, yoga teacher and coach, and the founder of Visit Peace, for a magazine article on well-being. As I've already confessed, I'm completely enamored by the name Visit Peace, because visiting peace is something so many of us aspire to do. And as Nousu and I began to chat, we connected on many levels as we realized we shared many common interests and experiences.

"Our current living environment and fast-paced lifestyle

are setting some real challenges for maintaining contact with who we are and the prerequisites for our health and well-being," Nousu told me.

"My key interest is to bring people back to this connection and help them find ways to take better care of themselves. This is also how we can better understand and help each other," said Nousu, whose surname means "rise" in Finnish.

Her own experiences with burnout and a rare endocrine disease set her on a journey of inquiry and career transition, with the goal of helping others.

When it comes to burnout, which the WHO recently classified as an occupational phenomenon in the International Classification of Diseases, I would venture to say that it's not exclusively work-related; people can burn out from simply having too much on their plate. As the borders between work and leisure fade, which we've witnessed during the pandemic but had already been under way with the shift toward the gig economy, the work lives of many people have changed.

According to the Lancet Commission on Global Mental Health and Sustainable Development, mental health disorders are on the rise throughout the world and will cost the global economy $16 trillion by 2030. The report, released in late 2018, recommends that mental health be reframed as a fundamental human right that promotes mental well-being, prevents mental health problems, and enables recovery from mental health disorders. According to the report, nearly two billion people suffer from mental illness every year.

Being burned out—for those who haven't experienced it—is like gradually finding yourself physically and mentally paralyzed. Not only can you lose your interest and ability to do the most basic things such as eating, but your body and mind can also stop functioning properly. It's as though you have been unplugged from your power source, but no matter what you do, you can't seem to find the right socket to recharge. Completing the simplest tasks can seem impossible. Physically, your exhausted body aches and you just want to go to sleep. Your motivation significantly wanes. It can all seem pointless. Even something as basic as having a conversation with a loved one or unloading the dishwasher can seem like an insurmountable task that requires Herculean effort.

One of the best descriptions of burnout I've come across is from the Finnish public mental health hub Mielenterveystalo.fi:

Exhaustion or burnout is a loud cry of distress from the body and mind, usually preceded by long-term pressure to perform that exceeds one's own resources. The body gradually becomes accustomed to an increasing load, from which, however, it is unable to recover sufficiently. Over time, this leads to failure of the body's regulatory systems, changes in central nervous system function, and the body finding it increasingly difficult to repair itself. Exhaustion is reflected in, among other things, fatigue for which rest does not help, the desire to withdraw from relationships, and problems with concentration and memory . . . it's common to try to persevere for years with poor strength and many symptoms.

• • •

NOUSU SAYS SHE founded her practice with the idea that when a person is burned out or stressed, it would be helpful to have a place where they could go and find experts from different areas ranging from physical therapy to coaching and perhaps even peer support groups under the same roof.

The motto of her center is *"kehon kautta mielenrauhaan,"* which roughly translates to "through, or using the body to create peace of mind."

"My dream was to create a center of empowerment that offers you what you need and is also serene and welcoming," Nousu tells me.

Sisu Through Healing

This concept of a center for empowerment is universal, for the importance of an all-encompassing approach to mind-body is key for healing and building resilience.

When it comes to treating the mind, talking about our troubles in professional therapy can be beneficial. Some people may dismiss therapy or find it scary or foreign. Yet if you have a twisted ankle or an unusual ache or pain, you go to the doctor. So if your mind or soul is troubled, why not seek professional help?

By talking with a professional, it's possible to unlock ways of thinking that aren't working for you, or to have revelations that in hindsight seem so obvious, yet no matter how many times you tried to process the issue in your mind, you couldn't resolve it.

Through both one-on-one and group therapy, you can often experience important revelations. A fresh, new perspective can help you better deal with whatever is on your plate. We all struggle. And when it comes to trauma, sharing your story and hearing about other people's similar experiences can help you feel less alone, less ashamed, and less broken.

In fact, Finland has set a goal to become the most therapy-positive country in the world. And that goal arose out of a serious challenge: a horrific security breach in 2020 in which thousands of psychotherapy patients were contacted by hackers who threatened to expose their details if they didn't pay up. But, instead, in a situation that turned around in a true example of sisu, public and private figures stood up on social media to say that they had gone to therapy and were proud of it. A new, pro-therapy movement was started.

I have greatly benefited from many forms of therapy, including psychotherapy and group therapy in the form of a several-week seminar for dealing with and healing in the aftermath of a relationship breakup.

It was my mother who noticed that I had put off grieving my divorce several years ago due to a busy stretch of work and life, and later, when I was blindsided by an unexpected sense of failure, grief, and sadness that was impacting my overall well-being, she suggested I needed help to process what had happened and would likely benefit from peer support.

As with so many things, my wise mother was absolutely right.

Taking the course, a Finnish version adapted partly from the late American author and family therapist Dr. Bruce Fisher's work, and dealing with the many unexpected emotions that arose post-divorce rather than trying to ignore them (truth be told, that approach wasn't working out so well for me) was both helpful and healing.

And just as valuable was connecting with other people who were going through similar experiences and realizing that my experiences and feelings were common.

While I use the example of divorce, it can be any difficult life event or un-dealt-with trauma. For example, think how much more alone you would have felt during the pandemic if you hadn't known that so many other people were going through the same things you were, feeling socially isolated at home in their sweatpants, wrestling with their own demons, and feeling anxious about the future. It's perfectly normal to feel pain and shame and then find solace and relief in discovering that other people share similar experiences and feelings.

There's also a feeling of comfort in sharing the small and large details of a breakup and realizing that whatever the parameters were, when shared with others who provide understanding and support, the load of emotional baggage and assorted feelings feels a little less awful.

During the seminar we go into our childhoods (yes, classic Freud), and by examining them, realize that if we grew up with an emotionally absent, abusive, or narcissistic parent, there may be an unconscious tendency to duplicate that pattern by seeking out a similar partner. For you may subconsciously seek out what is familiar without even being aware of it.

We learn that being aware of our own histories and issues and patterns sets us up to better develop resilience or sisu.

Another unexpected shock that happens to many people after a breakup is what I call the friendship shuffle. Post-breakup, there's a loss of contact with some people who have been part of your friendship group as a couple, and those who were your former spouse's friends. Sometimes this is natural, and maybe even a positive thing, if the friendship was based only on your previous partner's friendship with them. But there can also be unexpected friendship losses—people you thought would stand by you no matter what. When they disappear, it can cause additional pain, especially if you're already in a difficult place, and especially when you realize that some people you had considered close friends were actually available only for the good times, ready to share a glass of bubbly but not a flute full of sorrows. Those may also be the same people who rarely ask those three simple words: "How are you?"

• • •

ANOTHER STRONG ENDORSEMENT for therapy as a sisu builder is that very often the things we don't deal with have a way of coming back to haunt us. For example, someone who has experienced physical abuse in their childhood and not dealt with it may inadvertently carry on the same behavior patterns in discipling their own children. The cycle of abuse continues, which is incredibly unfair to the child and all those affected.

Dealing with your own issues, whatever they may be, is about caring for other people and for the world—it's a sisu-building action, for resilience comes from taking care of your own emotional baggage so that you don't inadvertently spill it onto others. While the goal of therapy is to help yourself, when you deal with your own issues, you become more self-aware and less likely to project those unresolved issues onto others.

And happily, through the seminar group I meet Peppi and Heli, two women with whom I became close friends—so much so that Peppi, who happens to live in my neighborhood, will check in on my son if I'm working late. We also often go for long strolls along the Helsinki seaside, walking and talking about whatever is on our minds. We have so many things in common, including a love of nature and its restorative powers.

• • •

WHEN IT COMES to care for the mind-body, the approach to understanding the relationship between the human body and mind as an integrated unit, Nousu, who calls herself "a full-time student of movement, mind, and the human being," holds that a balance of activities is important.

"Finns have traditionally had these inherent ways to calm down, relax, and find some quiet time such as the sauna, which is also communal; community is infinitely important, as is nature and being in the forest, as for many Finns urbanization arrived quite late," she says.

Before the Second World War, 75 percent of Finns lived in rural areas. Today, according to 2019 statistics, 85.45 percent of the population lives in cities and urban areas.

Digitalization has helped our lives in many ways, but the reality is that it has also greatly changed and influenced our attention spans, and the hours spent online contribute to our hypervigilant state, says Nousu. Pre-digitalization, after a day of doing physical work, we came back to the hut or home and calmed down by carrying out our evening routines together. "Now the world is very different. In the evenings it's grab a device, watch this Netflix series, and then go on social media for a bit, and answer some emails," she says.

Fortunately, we've started to pay attention to this and its effects. "I think where we are now, Lapinlahden Lähde, is a good example. On a large scale we give value to communality in the middle of a natural setting; there's a real sense of community with all kinds of hands-on activities and workshops to let people participate in experiences where they are physically and mentally present, not just staring at a screen," she says.

The slogan of Lapinlahden Lähde is "*kaikille avoin mielen hyvinvoinnin keidas,*" which roughly translates to "an oasis of mental well-being open to all."

Surrounded by nature and the sea, the center is housed in a two-hundred-year-old building that was once a hospital, built in 1841 by the czar's decree (Finland was then an autonomous grand duchy of Russia) as the first specialized psychiatric hospital in Finland. The main building was designed by architect Carl Ludvig Engel, who also designed other parts of Helsinki, including the magnificent buildings surrounding Senate Square, with its majestic Helsinki Cathedral, one of the most popular tourist spots in the Finnish capital.

The public mental health organization, now called MIELI Mental Health Finland, was founded at Lapinlahti back in 1897.

The values of Lapinlahden Lähde are openness, communality, and participation. Everyone is welcome to take part in events and workshops. Their slogan is "We contribute to society by preventing isolation and decreasing social exclusion."

• • •

IN HER PREVIOUS career, Nousu spent many years in the corporate world, including an eleven-year stint in IT at Nokia, the

Finnish telecom company that was once the world's leading mobile phone maker.

When Nousu first experienced the symptoms of burnout (before she knew what it was) she decided to take all of her holidays, overtime, and holiday pay as free time. It added up to many months as a voluntary sabbatical. "At the time I lived with my husband in Lauttasaari, a residential island in Helsinki, and during my time off I spent a lot of time outdoors in nature. I have this image of my head metaphorically opening up and the wind blowing through, airing it out and creating space for new ideas," she says.

After her sabbatical, Nousu returned to work and realized that she didn't know how to regulate or manage her energy, which became an area of interest.

When Helsinki was chosen World Design Capital in 2012, Nousu took on a job as a work-life designer for 925 Design (that's "nine-to-five," like the traditional workday), a Finnish company looking to create a more functional office working life. (This was pre-pandemic, when many more people worked in offices and traditional workplaces and workspaces.)

As Finland boasts an illustrious design heritage (think colorful prints in clothing and home textiles by Marimekko; timeless glass- and tableware by Iittala; and modernist spaces by designer and architect Alvar Aalto, Finland's Frank Lloyd

Wright), and one of the fundamentals of a good life is a sustainable, well-designed world, designing a healthier work-life balance makes perfect Nordic sense.

One of 925 Design's takeaways is *The Workbook*, a hands-on guidebook authored by visionaries and 925 founders Pekka Pohjakallio and Saku Tuominen. Though it was published over a decade ago, the text on the back cover resonates today: "Our work is confusing and fragmented; we feel busy all the time. We don't believe people feel overworked because they're doing too much work. A more likely reason is that they're doing too much work that feels meaningless and too little work that is meaningful."

Those words so aptly describe one of the emotional and physical states that accompany burnout: doing too much for the wrong reasons.

Energy, or Sisu Management

How you manage your energy is part of the key to building up resilience, a healthy sense of sisu.

How do you regulate your energy? When do you say, "No, this is too much"? Especially if you're in a situation at work, home, or another place where you don't feel you have the right or the option to say no? And how do you ensure that you have enough downtime to rest and recover from your job or jobs, especially in a world where the edges between work and play are increasingly blurry?

As a sensitive person, I've learned that I need to have time to recharge and gather my thoughts, or I can feel overwhelmed.

Nousu has a rare neuroendocrinological disease that was discovered when she was in her twenties following an extremely stressful life situation. She says that she was in constant fight-or-flight mode, which meant her adrenal glands were working overtime and there was more adrenaline than needed. Initially, it was taken care of with an operation. After the situation renewed itself, she became interested in the connection between illness and stress factors and how it's possible to influence your own health.

That led her to an interest in stress physiology. "My focus is on understanding and self-regulating the autonomic nervous system in order to avoid or recover from chronic stress and its consequent conditions," says Nousu.

She then poses an interesting question: "What does it mean to be healthy or to be sick? Can a person have peace of mind and balance even if they have an illness?" Many, many people have lifelong health conditions, and lifestyle can play a large role in their maintenance.

• • •

ONE OF THE workshops that Nousu teaches is a stress-release and management course that gives participants the tools to deal with and recover from daily stress. It's like an empowering sisu toolkit, with ways to maintain your everyday strength and resilience.

One of those skills is a focus on lifelong learning, which is a very Finnish approach.

"When you have learned body awareness and techniques for regaining that equilibrium, you will be better able to deal with challenging situations. Replacing old harmful patterns with new ways to restore mind and body are key. And just when you think you've figured out how to manage your life, a new situation comes along and you may inadvertently slide back into some of the old ways of coping that weren't working for you and need to find new ones," Nousu explains.

Continual learning in all its forms is another key to resilience, vitality, and happiness.

Some people in their seventies and eighties are far more dynamic, engaged, and interested in the world than people half their age. In part, this is because they continue to learn. They take piano lessons or German classes and participate in all manner of activities from exercise classes to swimming. Or start-ups. Case in point, a fellow winter-swimming friend of mine, a retired veterinarian, recently co-launched a new business that brings the healing sounds of music to hospital wards by offering art therapy in the form of visiting musicians who play live sets.

It's an all-encompassing approach, to tap into sisu and open-mindedly look at the world and continue to learn how to take care of yourself and others. Accept that nothing is fixed: life is like a flowing river, and changes and learning new things are part of the flow. When you stop, so does the flow.

Self-evaluation is important. "We need the techniques to observe, review, self-evaluate, and to get yourself out of the deep pits, the darkness, the difficult moments," says Nousu. "The answer doesn't always have to come from outside. It is in you and you can learn to listen to your body and trust the experience."

Nousu subscribes to the idea that everything in the universe is essentially inseparable and interconnected, which is so apt: when you take care of yourself, you are also taking care of the world.

• • •

AN INVALUABLE RESILIENCE-BUILDING skill is training yourself to be in the current moment, without worry or concern for any other moment. For those like me, who often feel as though they need to manage five hundred thoughts a minute, this is easier said than done.

Combine that with another reality, which is that the body remembers trauma. And un-dealt-with trauma can wreak havoc.

As Bessel van der Kolk writes in his seminal *New York Times* bestseller *The Body Keeps the Score*, the connection between mind and body, emotions and experiences, is incredibly strong.

According to van der Kolk, a Dutch-born psychiatrist, researcher, and author based in the United States who has spent much of his professional life studying how children and adults adapt to traumatic experiences, the body responds to extreme experiences by secreting stress hormones. While these hormones are often blamed for subsequent illness and disease, their original function was to give us strength and endurance to respond to extraordinary conditions and situations.

One of van der Kolk's findings is that people who proactively do something to deal with a disaster, whether it's transporting the injured to a hospital, being part of a first aid team, or preparing meals, utilize their stress hormones for the right purpose and therefore lower the risk of becoming traumatized.

Long after the traumatic experience is over, according to van der Kolk, it may be reactivated by the slightest hint of danger, which mobilizes disturbed brain circuits and causes massive amounts of stress hormones to be secreted.

This may lead to unpleasant emotions and sometimes intense physical sensations and post-traumatic reactions that can feel overwhelming. After trauma, the world is experienced with a different nervous system that has an altered perception of risk and safety.

In one of the examples, he cites the vagus nerve, which registers gut-wrenching feelings, and says that when a person becomes upset, their throat can become dry and their voice tense, while the heartbeat speeds up and breathing becomes rapid and shallow.

Reading his words reminds me of so many stories and anecdotes that I've heard about the long-term effects of trauma from bullying, whether it's in a workplace, in a relationship, or at school. Years later, traumatized people may avoid certain people, places, colors, and scents because the post-traumatic stress, anxiety, and fear associated with them are so great that they cause a mental and physical reaction.

• • •

ONE OF THE best places to release stress and even deal with trauma is in nature.

Though I grew up near fantastic forests and nature on the

west coast of Canada, I didn't fully appreciate or understand the brilliance, beauty, and restorative power of the woods until I moved to Finland.

In Finland, Europe's most forested country, more than 75 percent of the country is covered by trees. Forests are open around the clock and free to everyone, as the concept of everyman's right means anyone can walk, hike, camp, forage for berries or mushrooms in the forests, or swim in the lake or sea, as long as they behave respectfully.

Quite simply, the forest is a safe, happy, and restorative place to be. According to a 2018 survey, more than 80 percent of respondents in Finland said that the forest is important to them, as a safe place to be for walking, foraging, spending time at a cottage, or simply relaxing and having a connection to nature.

And nature is just about everywhere in Finland. According to Suomen Latu, the Outdoor Association of Finland, "for the average person living in Finland the natural environment is on average 200 meters away—and the doors are open 24-7."

I spotted a Finnish real estate ad featuring an image of a woman jogging in the forest with the words *"Kotiovelta lenkkipolulle,"* which roughly translates to "From your front door to the jogging trail," with much smaller photos of four different apartments and their descriptions, which take up about one-quarter of the space. This ad neatly reflected cultural values: the proximity to nature is much more important than the space indoors.

I've spent much time in the forests of Finland, from hiking paths in the greater Helsinki area to trails near lakeside cottages and wilderness routes in Lapland. As I walk in nature, in the forest, by parks, and by the sea, it's clear that it's a powerful form of self-prescription for healing, experienced both solo and with caring friends.

My dear friend Tiina sends me a handwritten Get Well Soon card by mail—a treat in these digital times—with an invitation for my son and me to come and spend the weekend with her and her husband at their home in the countryside about fifty kilometers (thirty-one miles) outside of Helsinki.

On the sweet card that Tiina sends, it says the program will include: "forest, sauna, relaxing, food, and autumn swimming." These are, I believe, the key elements of restoration and happiness. It's as simple as that. And indeed, they speak to the strong cottage or *mökki* culture in Finland—many people spend the holiday month of July and weekends and holidays at rustic cabins and cottages—where spending time relaxing in nature is the main event.

Tiina and I share a love of cold-water swimming, so naturally the weekend includes refreshing dips in the local lake.

We also go foraging for mushrooms, and I notice that my son, who is an awesome forager, is utterly full of joy as we pick mushrooms in the mossy forest.

As we have a post-foraging break in the forest, I'm convinced the coffee tastes better outdoors, as does the delicious chocolate roll cake that Tiina's husband, Juha, has baked for us.

On the Saturday night, we enjoy a good steam in their traditional wood-burning sauna. My son eagerly helps Juha chop the wood, an activity he loves so much that he chops several basketfuls of extra wood and offers to do more so they don't run out after the weekend.

This is nature therapy at its best.

Forest Bathing

I've spent much time in forests throughout my life, but it wasn't until my third and fourth decades that I really started tapping into their potential and thinking about how beneficial forest time is when it comes to well-being and happiness.

One of the stress-relieving exercises I do when I'm feeling utterly anxious is imagining that I'm lying on a soft moss-covered forest floor, when it's still warm out but there's an autumnal freshness in the air. In my imagination, as I look up at the majestic trees (the Earth's lungs) and their branches and leaves and imagine all of the life below me as the roots of the trees snake through the soil, my own problems seem small in comparison.

There is, of course, a long history of forest bathing or forest therapy in many cultures around the world from Japan to Finland, with scientific studies that show how simply going for a short walk in the woods can be beneficial to well-being.

The Outdoor Association of Finland's *Metsämieli*, or Forestmind, workshops, were created by Sirpa Arvonen in 2014, based on her book of the same name.

Essentially, Forestmind teaches a system of skills with exercises designed to utilize and intensify the natural healing effects of forests. It incorporates the newest and most widely accepted trends in psychology, therapy, and coaching, including mindfulness.

For example, just ten minutes in nature lowers your blood pressure, twenty minutes improves your mood, and an hour increases your attention span. After two hours, the body's defense mechanisms have increased, according to Arvonen's book.

When we met, Arvonen told me that she has been inspired by several leading positive psychology groundbreakers such as

Martin Seligman and Barbara Fredrickson, who is perhaps best known for her "broaden-and-build theory of positive emotions," which provides a blueprint for how pleasant emotional states, fleeting as they may be, contribute to resilience and well-being.

Arvonen tells me that when she experienced her own serious illness and the accompanying uncertainty, she was encouraged by friends to write down all that she had learned from the forest to share with others.

"Your resilience grows as nature accepts you just as you are, and you can develop self-regulation skills and improve your parasympathetic system by spending time in nature. The cycle of nature also teaches you about renewal and appreciation. When it's a dark November day, it's like hibernation and then the different seasons bring renewal and you have a totally different appreciation for the spring and summer after winter," she says.

"It's always worth going into the forest," Arvonen says. "It's a good way to deal with stress. For example, if you're facing a stressful situation, perhaps you need to go to the dentist, or for an operation, and you're feeling anxious, spending even ten minutes in the forest will bring down your stress levels."

She highlights the fact that there has been much research

in Finland and other parts of the world into the mental and physical health benefits of forest therapy, which is backed by evidence-based research.

Arvonen, an expert in behavioral sciences and well-being at work and the director for eHealth services at Helsinki University Hospital, also brings up something that I hadn't thought about but is so obvious in hindsight: time spent in the forest can also be about having honest, authentic conversations with others, about peer support and equality, as the forest is open to everyone. You don't need a special or expensive membership, you can come as you are, and for most people in Finland, it's nearby.

Arvonen points out that although there's been a boom in the popularity of the great outdoors, especially during the pandemic, when people were looking for safe social-distancing activities, there are people, even in Finland, who haven't grown up with a close relationship to the forest.

• • •

THERE'S A BEAUTIFUL nonjudgmental quality in nature.

I gained about ten kilos (more than twenty pounds) during my pandemic burnout episode and was in poor physical shape—just a short walk would leave me winded. But in the forest that didn't matter. I could walk for five or ten minutes, or an hour or two. Any option was completely acceptable. Whether I walk slowly or quickly, I am accepted as I am—the forest doesn't care what size I am—which I think is very important for anyone, particularly someone who is feeling low.

I asked Arvonen how she introduces the forest to newbies, and she tells me that a gradual introduction is best.

"We don't head off on a long, intense hike, we just start with a short visit to the woods or even to a nearby park, just somewhere that's green. We can just look around and be aware of how our senses activate. Then we practice taking deep breaths in and out and paying attention to how that feels," she explained.

She also described how people tend to talk very openly and honestly in the forest. Perhaps because there's less need to pretend to be something or focus on material or external things. This focus on authenticity is restorative.

"The goal is to make it as simple as possible," says Arvonen. Some of those activities are very basic, like leaning against a tree. How many times have you stopped to do that? "A tree is resilient; even though the wind blows, the tree stays standing even if it is swaying," she says.

Arvonen says that other very simple exercises, like asking

yourself and your fellow forest-goers "How are you?" provide a check-in and for many people an opening to chat and talk about how they're really feeling both mentally and physically.

One of the exercises Arvonen employs is asking participants to raise their fingers to indicate how they're doing. One hand represents the mind and the other the body. On a scale of one to five, participants can evaluate their physical and mental states.

When was the last time you paid attention to your fingers and hands, other than when using them to do work on a computer or complete a task? This is a good example of sharing, thinking, and using the mind-body connection.

Forest therapy is also a sisu-building skill, for resilience is increased by self-care.

Arvonen also emphasizes that if visiting a forest is not an option, a city park or even just a space with a lot of plants can provide a little green therapy.

The Art of Foraging

When it comes to Finnish forests, I meet the most fascinating people in them.

My son is wild about mushrooms and loves picking them.

But as I didn't grow up in Finland, I don't have the knowledge about which ones are edible that so many Finns seem to have, so I decided that the best thing would be for us to go on a guided foraging trip.

I found one online through Helsinki WildFoods and one autumn Sunday my son and I took the bus to Espoo, on the outskirts of Helsinki, where our guide, Anna Nyman, wearing a bright yellow raincoat, greeted us and the half dozen or so participants in the lush woods of Lakisto.

Nyman, who is a biologist and a wild food adviser, takes guided tours to the nearby forests of Helsinki, as there are enormous amounts of superfood growing in the forests, from wild herbs and vegetables to mushrooms.

At the start, Nyman had laid out a mushroom gallery for us on a mossy embankment, the soft carpet of the forest, with several different types of mushrooms and their names on re-usable laminated labels.

She started by giving us a brief overview and suggested that we focus on one or two particular mushroom families rather than trying to take everything in all at once.

Nyman observed, "Often in the beginning, when people are foraging, they'll say that they're not finding mushrooms as they rush through the woods. But when they slow down and stop for a bit, suddenly they can see mushrooms everywhere."

When you slow down, you see the stars.

This seems like good advice in general, for when you slow down, you see the stars.

As we headed off to look for mushrooms after the introduction, Nyman assured us not to worry, she'd check what we found to ensure that there were no dangerous mushrooms in our baskets.

Chatting with our fellow foragers, I met Roberta Lima, an accomplished Brazilian-born Austrian video and performance artist living in Finland. As we talked, she told me how since moving to Finland, she had developed a new relationship to nature, which was something that growing up in Brazil she didn't have, as forests and nature were often something to be scared of. For her, spending time in nature and learning to forage for mushrooms, for example, was a totally new experience and one that informed her art.

Her video "Beyond the Box by Roberta Lima," which is viewable on YouTube, shows the making of *Ghost Plant* (2020), where the text at the start of the video reads:

"Inspired by incredible structures existing in nature and our surroundings, this work is a representation of systems of support and connectivity. In the forest, trees of different species have been thought to fight for light, but in reality they benefit from one another when sharing the same space. Their intertwined roots and a symbiotic relationship to fungi create an underground economy that exists beneath trees: a huge network, called 'The Wood Wide Web.'"

As we chat, Lima asks something that several people have asked me: "What about feminism and sisu?"

Long after our initial meeting, her question stayed with me, and later, it set me on a journey that I've since been on for a long time. It's also another example of nature bringing like-minded souls together.

CHAPTER 4
. . . .

BETTER TOGETHER

The Power of Helping Sisu and Community in Solving Problems

S TEPPING INTO THE Brooklyn Cafe, tucked into the heart
of Helsinki's hip Punavuori neighborhood, is like taking a
mini-trip to its namesake, one of New York City's coolest
boroughs.

Owned and run by sisters Brenda and Sharron Todd, the
café serves up a range of popular North American favorites,
from delicious iced cupcakes to generous bagel sandwiches
and Oreo milkshakes. And, of course, dark-roasted coffee,
which they call "a little brightness in a cup." There's also a
small library nook with a selection of secondhand classics, re-
flecting the sisters' love of literature.

In early 2020, pre-pandemic, the sisters put out a social

media post that shocked many of their loyal Helsinki patrons when they announced that they were facing bankruptcy. But it wasn't because their business wasn't doing well—it was actually quite profitable, with a more than 25 percent profit margin—it was because they had some unpaid start-up debts that were threatening their livelihood.

Within seventy-two hours, the public made donations through a crowdfunding initiative on Mesenaatti.me, Finland's first and largest crowdfunding platform, and a donor stepped forward offering to pay off their debts.

Intrigued and inspired, I reached out to the sisters, for this seems like a perfect example of supportive sisu, when people come together to help others deal with a big-time challenge or setback. Little did I know that the sisters would teach me more about sisu than I knew.

• • •

WHEN I FIRST met Sharron and Brenda, who moved from Brooklyn, New York, to the Finnish capital in 2011 to set up shop, we chatted about how it felt when locals and loyal patrons stepped up to support independent café ownership and counter the trend of large chains taking over, which is happening around the world.

"We were completely blown away and honored; many of

our customers said that they wouldn't just let us leave so easily, and asked if they couldn't at least help us fight to stay open," says Brenda.

"It came as a total, but wonderful, surprise," says Sharron. "We had already come to terms with the fact that we would have to close up shop. It felt as though the whole city had come together to show that they cared."

This idea, this feeling of community sisu, of fighting for what you believe in and stepping in to help others, is part of the way forward. For if we don't help one another and take a stand or offer to help when someone or something is flailing, what's the point?

Brooklyn Sisu

As we chat about resilience and the strange liberating power that follows after you think you've lost something that you've worked so hard for and accepted it, they tell me that one of their favorite Finnish words is *sisu*.

I ask them what their definition is. "Sisu is having a combination of courage, grit, and integrity. It's being able to persevere despite your circumstances and what life has thrown your way," they replied together.

The sisters, who have a Korean mother and a Black American father, have lived in Seoul, Brooklyn, California, Virginia, and Rome. We quickly bonded over being from many different places and cultures and having an intercultural perspective, seeing things in many different ways compared to a monocultural mindset, the idea that there is only one correct way to do things.

I identify with being an outsider, or perhaps more accurately an insider-outsider. Although I speak Finnish (albeit with a slight accent) and understand many social norms and behaviors because I've lived here for more than a decade, I often question set cultural behaviors or norms from a slightly different perspective than the locals.

It's only as an adult that I've learned to value not fitting in, being a bit weird and different. For a human being and a writer, it's a huge asset. From an empathy perspective it's also been very useful, because although I do fit into many categories, I often don't fit into the mainstream and can sympathize with, relate to, and understand others who don't.

Ultimately, embracing being different is something that helps to build sisu.

"Our experiences set us up with resilience, but they also set us apart in Finland, because when people are talking about things, they're often talking about them within the confines of their own culture, their own country," said Sharron, who worked for many years as a Korean cryptological linguist with the US Army Military Intelligence Corps, reporting to the NSA, the National Security Agency. She also spent more than a decade working in the high-powered human resources world in New York.

I have long held the view that if more people were truly bi- or trilingual and had experiences of living in different countries and cultures, there would (perhaps) be fewer wars and conflicts, as people would see that there are many ways to do things and that one way or cultural norm is not necessarily the right or only way.

When it comes to a concept such as sisu, having an insider-outsider view is very useful, for the broadness an international view offers. I've met many Finns who have an outdated or limited view of sisu, partly because there's an assumed static definition based on history that hasn't been updated.

Several of the people vested in the concept, such as the world's leading sisu researcher, Emilia Elisabet Lahti, have spent much time studying, living, and working outside Finland, which has likely offered many other perspectives, culturally, academically, and personally.

I asked the Todd sisters whether they think their cultural understanding translates into a greater overall sense of empathy in other aspects of life, such as age, gender, orientation, race, and socioeconomic status.

"Definitely. Absolutely," replied Brenda, who has twenty years of experience in gastronomy and the restaurant industry.

"And sometimes to a fault; it's almost deafening, because for lack of a better word when you're in an argument or discussion about a political issue or a social issue, it's easier to see almost all the sides," Sharron said.

"But truly, not for the sake of playing devil's advocate, but because we can see all the different points of view," Brenda noted.

"And it's not a middle-of-the-road thing either," added Sharron.

"I'll firmly take a stand," said Brenda. "But it's so nuanced and I know why you're coming from that perspective of 'But what about this and this and this?'"

"And it can keep you on the outside, and you can take that negatively, and sometimes it's lonely there," said Sharron.

As we discussed resilience, I asked them what their sisu-building advice is. What it is that allows some people to push ahead while others place blame for their misfortunes on other people or circumstances?

"Not having self-pity!" answered Sharron, and the sisters laughed.

"It's a Todd family thing—we're allergic to pity. We're so grateful that our parents raised us to not take things for granted. Especially our mom wouldn't show pity for superficial things even if she maybe felt it, but we knew she had our back when it came to the big things. As a kid, if someone laughed at my shoes, she was like 'So?' Or if someone said my nose was too big, she would say, 'The world can be unkind and sometimes people are going to feel entitled to make those comments, so if you give people a license, by, one, believing them in the first place, or, two, feeling sorry for yourself, you're going to have a really tough life,'" said Sharron.

"You can still cry into your pillow but at the end of the day you have to go back to school in the morning with your head held high and not let other people's comments affect your identity, your self-worth, or your confidence," added Brenda.

Their advice for building up resilience: "Get outside of your comfort zone, broaden your experiences, and get over yourself. The sooner you get over yourself, the better, because the world needs you and desperately," said Sharron.

One technique they recommend, which I wholeheartedly endorse, is self-evaluation, which means taking a long, hard look at your own actions. "We do it hourly; when you're running a business and dealing with employees and customers, we often ask ourselves, 'Was I a little too sharp?'" Sharron explained. "Accountability is the key foundation to building resilience. So often people focus on what other people are doing wrong," she added.

Trying to consider the other person's point of view, even when people are downright hurtful or rude, though difficult, can be constructive.

In addition to self-evaluation and accountability, there's the importance of seeing the bigger picture. "I'm sure every child's parent has said, 'Finish your food, there's children starving in the world,'" said Brenda. She gives the example of a water main break in her apartment building, which put her in a bad mood, until she reminded herself that there are a lot of people in the world without potable water, not to mention a warm apartment, access to a hot shower, and electricity.

Some people spend a lot of time feeling that they've been dealt an unfair hand in life, perhaps without realizing that challenges are part of the human condition.

"Somewhere along the way somebody told someone that life, if you were nice and made all the right decisions, was going to be easy. I don't know who gave people that impression because life is literally challenges and overcoming them, it's a part of living. So then if your resilience, one of the most important life skills, is not sharpened, you end up with a whole bunch of really unhappy people, and unhappy people do really mean things to other people—they're bullies," said Sharron.

As Brenda so aptly put it: "Being kind is always in style."

Solving Big-Picture Issues

There is another news story on the topic of helping sisu, one that has a wide reach and massive global potential—and it's an excellent example of thinking outside the box, of looking at a serious societal challenge that affects so many of us from a fresh perspective.

In a nutshell, Helsinki has addressed the issue of homelessness with a very simple solution: by giving homes to homeless people. Which, on balance, makes so much sense.

Finland, instead of brushing the homelessness problem under the carpet and hoping it would go away, founded a successful national program with funding from the state for cities and many players including the Y-Foundation, a national developer of the Housing First principle, which provides affordable rental housing for the homeless. And lest it seem that this is a costly Nordic welfare state solution, it actually saves taxpayers money in the long run, as the medical and social costs of homelessness are high for society.

Finland is the only European Union member state country where homelessness is falling. In typical Finnish fact-loving and honest fashion, there are exact statistics and the admission that the homeless problem has not been solved entirely: there are still about 4,341 homeless people per 2021 statistics in Finland, which has a population of 5.5 million. But the situation, compared with many years ago, when there were tens of thousands of homeless in the country, is much improved.

Based on the findings of a working group report, a Finnish national program to reduce long-term homelessness was launched in 2008, with state, municipal, and NGO backing. Apartments were bought and converted into permanent housing.

The idea, which on both a national and an international level seemed radical at the time, was that housing is a basic human right. If a human being is in a tough place in their life, they need a home and help.

Many of those who are homeless are dealing with multiple issues such as trauma, poor mental and physical health, addiction, and personal losses, whether family or job related. Imagine dealing with those types of challenges while sleeping on the streets.

Reading *A Home of Your Own*, the handbook of the Y-Foundation, which runs this innovative program, I'm struck by the humanity of it all. In it, the Y-Foundation's current CEO, Juha Kaakinen, quotes English essayist, novelist, and critic George Orwell: "Either we all live in a decent world, or nobody does."

· · ·

FINLAND'S HOUSING FIRST program does cost money, of course, but according to a report by the Ministry of the Environment, the cost savings of taking a homeless person off the streets is about €15,000 (about $18,200) per person a year. That's based on calculations of services such as emergency health care, social services, and the justice system that the homeless don't use when they have homes.

In a show of sisu, Finland spent €250 million (about $300 million) creating new homes and hiring hundreds of extra support systems. But in the long term, the savings have outweighed the costs.

Part of the City of Helsinki's mixed housing formula aims to limit social segregation. In every new district, the city's formula is 25 percent social housing, 30 percent subsidized purchase, and 45 percent private sector. Incidentally, this mix appears in many neighborhoods throughout Finland, so there are fewer communities where everyone is of the same socio-economic background.

The Importance of Trust

For the Y-Foundation, two very important sisu-esque values stand out in their mission statement: courage and trust, which are also two fundamental Finnish qualities.

The foundation defines courage as follows: "We have the courage to be on your side even when others are not. We lead the way, make decisions and put our plans into action with an open mind." As for trust, "We do what we promise. Our tenants can trust in the affordability, continuity and safety of their housing."

In Finland, there is also high trust in fellow citizens and government. Trust has been highlighted in the *World Happiness Report 2020* as a quality that leads to better well-being. According to the report, good social support networks, social trust, honest government, safe environments, and healthy lives make up well-being.

One of the simple joys of living in Finland is that if you agree to meet a friend on a certain day and at a specific time, they'll very likely be there, on the dot. There's no need to send extra messages or call to see if you're still on.

If someone says they're going to help you, they will. And the same goes for work. Though of course it's advisable and sensible to get a contract, as a freelancer I know that for the most part, I can totally rely on what's been agreed upon verbally. This isn't true in every country or community—but it should be.

• • •

THERE'S AN IDEA that neatly sums up the reasoning behind giving homes to the homeless in Helsinki. Credited to former Helsinki mayor Jan Vapaavuori, who was previously Finland's housing minister, it's essentially this: The thinking used to be that people needed to get sober in order to be able to live in a flat or a home. But then the thinking was turned around: You need an apartment or a home in order to get sober.

In Finland, there is a long history, dating back to the 1980s, with the state, volunteers, municipalities, and NGOs working together to reduce homelessness. It's important to acknowledge that none of this happened overnight and that all of the actors had the same goal, which was to humanize the life of the homeless. This is forward-thinking, empathetic, and powerful sisu in action.

CHAPTER 5

· · · · · · · · · · ·

PEACEFUL NEGOTIATION SISU

How to Deal with Challenging People and Bullies

ONE OF MY sisu superpowers is dealing with difficult people.

This is not a skill that I have arrived at easily. It's the result of a lifetime of learning through the school of hard knocks, therapy, and supportive friends and family who have encouraged me to stand up for myself even when it has felt as though life situations (or certain people) were getting the better of me.

Navigating with challenging people is also the result of observing and learning how others manage and negotiate conflict.

Around lunchtime on an overcast day in November, I was

in a large grocery store in an upscale neighborhood in Helsinki's city center when I heard someone talking in a very loud voice before starting to yell. In all the years I've lived in Finland, I don't think I've ever heard anyone yelling in a grocery store in the middle of the day.

Startled, I turned around. A tidily dressed customer in his late sixties or early seventies was shouting at the female employee behind the fish counter. Along with several other customers, I moved closer. Though I wasn't sure what was happening, I was concerned for the woman's safety, as the man was so enraged that he was waving his arms over and around the counter and aggressively telling the woman behind it shut up.

As another customer approached the yelling man and told him it was totally unacceptable to talk to another person that way, the woman's younger, male coworker behind the fish counter stepped beside her and held up his hand to signal "stop." He calmly told the angry customer in polite, formal Finnish, "You are no longer being served here. Please be so kind as to leave."

The disgruntled man continued to voice complaints and hurl insults but, to our relief, started walking away.

I almost felt like clapping as a sense of relief washed over me, for the situation was anxiety-inducing on many levels.

Processing what happened, I felt admiration for the young man who stepped in and stood up for his coworker so diplomatically.

The point is not whether the customer was right or wrong, but that yelling, threatening, and insulting another person is definitely not the way to go. Apparently, the aggrieved customer was upset because the wrong piece of salmon was being selected, and when he decided to reach over the counter to indicate which fish he wanted and was asked not to do so for hygiene reasons, he became enraged.

I'm fascinated by the fact that several people immediately got involved in an effort to defuse and resolve the situation, but also to make it clear to the angry man that his behavior was totally unacceptable.

In a nutshell, what played out illustrates several of the effective approaches for how to deal with difficult people who are bullying others: in a calm manner, by setting boundaries and working together.

Dealing with Bullies

From my own experience as an individual and a parent, I know that it can take years to erase the feelings of worthlessness, self-doubt, and pain that follow long-term bullying, especially if you've been repeatedly belittled and berated.

Subsequently, it doesn't matter how many people say things that are the polar opposite of what the bully said, there's still a small heartachy wound that can be easily triggered.

An international study in 2020 published in *The Lancet* surveyed data from 220,000 students between the ages of twelve and fifteen in eighty-three countries and found that bullying causes suicidal behavior in more than one out of eight young people.

Together Sisu

"Together" is one of the cornerstones of the City of Helsinki's new anti-bullying program for elementary and secondary schools. Introduced in December 2020, KVO-13 roughly translates to "13 anti-bullying guidelines or actions."

When it comes to education, Finland has fared well in many international comparisons, including the Organisation for Economic Co-operation and Development's Programme for International Student Assessment, which tests fifteen-year-olds around the world on their reading, math, and science skills to address real-life challenges.

The Finnish public school system has also been much studied internationally, for a variety of reasons, including the fact that schoolkids in Finland often outperform their peers in many other countries—even though school systems in other countries are considered to be stricter and more rigorous.

Kids start school at age seven in Finland, and they have shorter school days and more free time than kids do in many other countries. For example, in elementary school, for every forty-five minutes of instruction, there is a fifteen-minute recess, which is usually outdoor play in the schoolyard. With Finland's high literacy rate, students also learn invaluable skills at elementary school, such as how to spot fake news and disinformation.

Education in Finland is virtually free (of course, we pay taxes) and accessible to everyone from day care through university. That means if a child is musically talented, they have the possibility of attending one of the country's top music schools, the Sibelius Academy, simply because of talent and drive, not because of money or connections.

A strong sense of equality carries over into the anti-bullying program. One of the KVO-13 program's tenets is founded on striving for a level playing field, which means that everyone is responsible for speaking out and stepping in when they witness bullying—not just the teacher or the kids involved, but the parents and the community as well. Which makes so much sense, as bullying often has far-reaching roots that affect many, many people. Numerous studies have shown that kids who have been bullied are at far greater risk for depression and suicide.

Quite simply, bullying begets bullying, and unfettered little bullies grow up to become big bullies.

One of the key architects behind the KVO-13 anti-bullying program is Vesa Nevalainen, a soft-spoken psychologist whose official title with the city is "pupil welfare services manager." Perhaps a more apt description of his role would be that he's tasked with the mental well-being of kids and youth in the high-quality public school system, which covers the large majority of students, as there are very few private schools in the capital city—or in Finland, for that matter.

Nevalainen has a long, varied career in anti-bullying work and has authored or coauthored more than half a dozen books on the topic, including *Ikävät Ihmiset: Kuinka Selviytyä Hankalien Tyyppien Kanssa* ("Unpleasant People: How to Cope with Difficult Types") and *Jo Riittää: Irti Kiusaamisesta ja Kiusaajista* ("Enough Already: Getting Rid of Bullying and Bullies"), two books whose titles speak directly to their hands-on approach.

Nevalainen described the Finnish approach of involving

and tasking everyone with the responsibility of curbing bullying. "It's a very ambitious strategy," he said. One of the main differences from previous programs is this shift toward a community focus. With KVO-13, the onus is on everyone to help, not just the teacher and the parents or guardians of the bullied and the bully. It's a societal problem, something that goes far beyond the school.

Supportive Sisu

"We can't do this on our own, we need all the outside help possible," said Nevalainen, who told me that feedback from students of all ages was instrumental in developing KVO-13. The program offers a "toolkit for the prevention of bullying" and has the goal of making the anti-bullying concept a common cause for the entire Finnish capital, with guidance for intervention and aftercare.

Introduced in December 2020, with the "13" in the title referring to the specific number of measures for addressing the problem of bullying, the program starts by gauging well-being indicators in schools and educational institutions and the individual well-being of each student. A school health survey and a well-being profile are maintained for each student; these are used by every school to monitor the daily lives and coping skills of pupils.

Part of KVO-13 is linked to programs that develop social-emotional learning (SEL), and in some schools SEL is a subject. Simplified, SEL is a methodology that helps students to better understand and manage their emotions and practice empathy toward others.

One of the cornerstones of this new anti-bullying approach links neatly back to the very foundation of Finnish society, which is based on the idea that how a society treats its weakest members is a measure of its humanity and civilization. In Finnish, the word *sivistys* refers to both civilization and education.

When I asked Nevalainen whether he thinks this is a Finnish quality—that is, looking out for and taking care of the most disenfranchised—he quickly replied that he's not a nationalist in any way, but concedes that the very fabric and basis of Finnish society is to help the weaker. He told me that he was drawn to a career in helping others because his own background was weak; when he was young, he got ahead because of help and therefore wanted to help others.

When it comes to helping sisu, this is another characteristic that I often notice in people who are helpers—they have received help and want to pay it forward.

One of my most pressing questions, in addition to getting practical anti-bullying advice, was: Why do people bully others?

"There are many reasons, but among the most common are anger, fear, and envy," replied Nevalainen. "Anger may be expressed through insults that are actually projections of their own insecurities, fears, or jealousy onto others. Or they may be trying to exert power over others because inside they feel powerless," he says, adding that if someone is different, kids and adults can feel threatened by it.

This matches with my own theory, which is that it's human nature for people to be focused on themselves, not always intentionally self-centered, but perhaps slightly less able to consider the world from someone else's vantage point. And through the prism of their own experiences, opinions, and emotions, they project onto others. If they're feeling insecure, they may take it out on others.

It's been well documented in many studies on bullying that being different somehow threatens some people. Whether it's your skin color, your sexuality, your career choice, or being outside the perceived norms, it can feel like a threat to those who live within societal expectations.

Though bullying decreased in the 2010s in primary and

secondary schools in Helsinki, according to a THL (the Finnish Institute for Health and Welfare) survey, as of 2019, one in three fourth- and fifth-graders and one in four eighth- and ninth-graders were likely to be bullied at school. Eight percent of primary-school children and 5 percent of secondary-school children are repeatedly bullied, every week.

Bullying in school has negative effects on a child's well-being and development resulting in poorer school performance, which can lead to depression and anxiety.

One of the best sets of advice for dealing with bullies that I find comes from KiVa (named for the Finnish word for "nice"), an earlier anti-bullying program developed by the Finnish Ministry of Education and Culture:

Be assertive. Communicate with your whole body that you will not accept bad treatment. Stand tall, look the bully in the eye and speak with a clear voice that what you are experiencing feels bad and it should stop immediately. It can work as the first step to stop that situation. If possible, act like you don't care, try to walk away from the situation and go tell someone about the situation. Every bullying situation is different and there is not a single right solution. These all are just suggestions you can try to do by yourself. It is important to tell someone about bullying: don't keep it to yourself!

This last line is so important, because being teased or bullied can make you feel defenseless and fill you with shame. The power of sharing your experience, whether you're eight, eighteen, twenty-eight, forty-eight, or eighty-eight years old, is key. Shame can make you want to crawl under a rock, to hide yourself away and isolate.

And as Nevalainen writes, it's important to acknowledge that even after the bullying, the pain doesn't just disappear: "Every time a bully is present, your self-confidence can dip to zero."

Simply acknowledging this fact is part of self-preservation sisu. Resilience is built by being aware of your weak spots and trying to minimize them.

I discuss this idea with my son, who tells me that he totally ignores and avoids his former bully. The fact that my son has had a growth spurt and is taller and bigger than his former bully has helped. But what do you do when that's not the case?

I have to deal on a semi-regular basis with a few bullies. Simply wishing them all the best and cutting them out of my life is not an option. However, what I have found helpful is to acknowledge that a lot of what they are bullying me about actually has to do with their own (unresolved) issues.

I found a sense of sisu when I realized, through the help of family and friends and therapy, that I was fully justified in setting boundaries and limiting contact. For example, instead of accepting potentially angry or triggering phone calls, I try to minimize transactions and deal with the things that need to be dealt with via text messages.

I also recognize a quality in myself that Nevalainen addresses in his work: the bullied may unknowingly repeat a sad formula in which they try to please others because they fear that they will be rejected.

It took me ages to realize that there was little point in spending time and effort trying to please some people, who seem to be forever disappointed, critical, and full of complaints about whatever I do. It's much more constructive to put that energy elsewhere.

Another message from Nevalainen's work is that bullying can lead to a deep sense of loneliness, as it feels as though no one understands the pain and suffering. A 2019 article from Yle, the Finnish national broadcaster, backs that up: "Previous research has shown that young people who are bullied experience more mental health symptoms, with the majority of the symptoms being found in adolescents who were bullied at school or online."

Another few lines from the article stand out: Andre Sourander, a professor of pediatric psychiatry at the University of Turku, is quoted as saying, "Young people with mental health problems are more susceptible to bullying and, on the other hand, being bullied exposes a person to mental health problems. This is important information for the development of school mental health and bullying interventions."

Practical Tips

If there is universal sisu advice for dealing with difficult people at any age, it is as follows: Limit contact and don't engage. This can be difficult, but for many people who have been abused or traumatized, any contact with the bully can be devastating. You don't need to be a nice person and engage with a toxic person and forsake yourself.

If there are issues that need to be resolved, get things in writing, especially if your bully is inconsistent, unreliable, prone to angry outbursts, or a this-needs-to-be-done-right-this-moment type. When you move to messaging, you have things in writing, but you also have the right to say that you'll get back to them, which gives you time to calmly think about whatever the issue at hand is. After all, there are few things that need to be done right this minute.

Don't try to convince them to see things your way. This can be a waste of energy. Listen, but stand your ground.

Don't personalize, even if you're attacked personally. Resist the temptation to do the same, because with bullies it's futile. Some bullies are actively looking for conflict, and when you don't play, the match is over.

Try to keep communications to the matter at hand, whether dealing with a difficult employee or with your boss, neighbor, or family member. Talk about the work, the project, the issue, the child's well-being, the legal document, the thing that needs to be taken care of, but don't get personal. If they attack you personally, don't take the bait. Bring the conversation back to the issue.

Try to consider things from their perspective, and remember that bullies often behave the way they do out of fear, anger, envy, and an inability to see any point of view other than their own. They may not be able to see the consequences of their own actions, for example, if they were raised in an environment where anger and insults were used to communicate; that is their modus operandi.

Though it's not classified as bullying per se, I've also come to consider indifference, which can be as harmful as hate, on par. It's not that I expect sympathy or compliments and praise from everyone, but I've started to pay close attention to indifference and, whenever possible, try to minimize contact with the indifferent. This is, of course, easier said than done, but life is a bit too short to spend with people who simply don't care.

My motto is to go toward the light—toward the empathetic, supportive, and caring people—whenever possible.

Sisu Superpowers

One of the teachers at my son's school tipped me off to an invaluable resource and source of sisu, a lovely Finnish book called *Hyvä Tyyppi: Supervoimien Käsikirja*, which roughly translates to "The Handbook of Superpowers for Cool Kids." Written by Merja Kalm with delightful illustrations by Mira Mallius, the book, which is used by the school, is about how to be resilient and help and stick up for others.

One of the spreads features a test titled *"Löytyykö sinusta sisua?"* which translates to: "Do you have sisu?" or "Can you find sisu within yourself?" There, young readers can assess their resilience in different challenging situations, along with a message that if they don't score high, it doesn't matter because sisu is a skill that can be practiced and learned, something that grows through action and practice.

One of the book's suggestions is that if you miss the last bus, you just strap your knapsack on your back and head off, as three kilometers is not such a long distance to walk. This to me seems like such a good example of sensible and simple sisu.

Other examples include taking a deep breath if you get upset and thinking before you do anything. Or if you fail, try again, because the next time will likely be more successful.

Teaching children how to be resilient and pivot in challenging times, rather than pitying them or instilling a victim mentality, is a great way to build sisu.

Listening

In my previous life, I traveled around the world for many years as a travel writer. One of the things I observed aboard flights was how well the staff handled difficult situations with demanding passengers. I spoke with a head purser for Finnair, the Finnish national airline, about how they're trained to cope with these challenging situations. The response was that it's almost always about trying to discuss a situation with the passenger. "That means listening to what they're upset about and trying to respond to that. Giving them the opportunity to talk about and express what's bothering them and then trying to figure out a solution together goes a long way to helping to diffuse the situation," she said.

Working together and finding compromises has a long history in Finland. A major milestone of Finnish diplomacy dates back to the post–Cold War years when Finland had to appease its big neighbor (then the Soviet Union, now Russia) next door while dealing with the rest of the world. As Finland shares a 1,300-kilometer border (about 807 miles) with its eastern neighbor, working together and finding solutions is nonnegotiable.

It wasn't until Finland joined the European Union in 1995, along with Austria and Sweden, that the country really signaled its move away from the east toward the west.

Throughout its history, Finland has played the role of peacekeeper internationally and has often been an intermediary, a peace broker, between east and west by hosting high-level political summits such as those between American and Russian presidents.

It's a sort of peaceful negotiation sisu—one that we can still learn from today.

CHAPTER 6

SOCIAL CHANGE SISU

Empowered Female Resilience

MANY YEARS AGO, when I moved from Canada to Finland, I felt a sense of relief, as though I had gained a voice as a person, an individual defined less by my gender and my appearance and more by my abilities.

This was a bit naive on my part, for there's still a lot of work to be done on the equality front in Finland and things are far from perfect. But from a feminist sisu perspective, my sigh of relief was in part due to my arrival in an environment that has a long legacy of striving for equality.

Finland was the first European country to give women full and parliamentary voting rights, which it did in 1906. There is generous paid maternity leave and support in practical forms such as virtually free, high-quality day care, which means that mothers—and fathers, for that matter—can have successful careers while their children are being well taken care of.

Add to that the famous baby box, the new-baby starter kit given to all expectant parents in a tradition that is more than eighty years old. It contains about fifty quality items, ranging from a baby sleeping bag to clothing and bibs, that are useful in a baby's first year. We still have the soft-haired brush that came with our baby box, which doubles as a newborn crib with a foam mini-mattress, more than ten years ago.

Employment rates for women and men are almost on par: according to 2019 statistics the employment rate in Finland for women was 71.8 percent and for men it was 73.3 percent, which ranks high in international comparisons.

When my son was little and in the daycare system, I marveled at how functional, positive, and instructive it was. In addition to having breakfast served in the morning and learning how to socialize with other children, with the emphasis on play, which is what children should do when they're young, my son participated in a range of educational and constructive activities, from baking to painting and spending time outdoors every day in the playground, no matter what the weather. Bundling up and heading out to play even when the mercury drops below zero is a great sisu-building exercise that teaches kids resilience from an early age. It's just a question of having the right gear, such as a warm snowsuit and hat and gloves.

Day care and preschool were far from a babysitting service; they were places where my son learned a range of practical life skills in a nourishing, safe environment with trained childcare professionals.

Women Lead

When it comes to women's rights and representation, as I write, Finland is ruled by a five-party female-led coalition government with Prime Minister Sanna Marin at its helm.

This has been rejoiced around the world with media headlines such as "Feminism Comes of Age in Finland" (BBC), which in addition to showing the way also sets the tone for girls and young women, who see that they too can be world political leaders.

There's a history of strong female leaders; Finland elected a female president in 2000 with Tarja Halonen, a popular leader who served two consecutive terms, for twelve years. And as early as 1926, Finland's first female minister was Miina Sillanpää, who became second minister of social affairs.

In the Finnish language, the gender-neutral pronoun *hän*

refers to both "he" and "she"; it's an inclusive pronoun that stands for equality. There is no "she" or "he."

• • •

WHEN IT COMES to female political leaders, there is a unique quality in Finnish prime minister Sanna Marin. She appears to be an idealist, one who builds bridges rather than focuses on differences. This is an attitude that I think represents a Finnish way of doing things, particularly in politics, where a five-party coalition government makes it a necessity to find compromises. But I also think it's partly a feminist approach. Women are used to negotiating and soothing ruffled feathers.

In her politics, Marin represents the ideal of striving for equality, whether that's gender based, socioeconomic, or other. The focus on perceived celebrity status or income and the idea that someone is somehow better because they are famous or rich seems passé in Finland.

This is also part of a sisu mindset: a down-to-earth humbleness in which everyone is treated equally—as people. In early 2021, when *Time* magazine chose Marin as one of the "next 100 most influential people," the headline for her profile said it all: "Finland's Sanna Marin, the World's Youngest Female Head of Government, Wants Equality, Not Celebrity."

This captures the Nordic ideal, one of the reasons the Nordics top the world happiness indexes. It's refreshing to read about a political leader who is using her power to focus on equality and sustainability and other values rather than on promoting her own image or fame.

According to the Global Gender Gap Report by the World Economic Forum for 2021, Iceland and Finland are the top countries for women's rights and opportunities. Iceland leads, and Finland follows.

Women of Sisu

On a wintry Sunday afternoon, I joined sisu researcher Emilia Elisabet Lahti at a meeting of her Women of Sisu group. That meeting, in the cozy home of one of the kind souls who belong to the group, started me on a journey of exploring the relationship between feminism and sisu.

I should say that I've received many messages from readers around the world asking for my take on feminism and sisu, but it was not until several things happened, including an afternoon with the Women of Sisu, that I started to delve into the topic.

My Finnish-born mother raised me to be independent; I

recall her saying to me at a very early age, "I don't care if you marry a millionaire, you need to have your own career, earn your own money, and be able to support yourself."

At the time—the early eighties in North America—that was a very strong message. Not that I ever dated or married a millionaire, but her point carried a feminist message about independence that reflected generations of independent, educated women in our family who have had careers ranging from nursing to pharmacy to dentistry.

I grew up in North America at a time when it was still not uncommon for some women to go to university to "earn their Mrs."—that is, find a husband to support them.

The Sisu Circle

There were about a half dozen of us and we started by sitting in a circle, and Lahti, who is such a source of light and inspiration, guided us through a session, where everyone had the opportunity to talk about what was on her mind.

There was a warmth, acceptance, and trust in the group that was so nourishing. With the exception of Lahti, I had not met the other women before. Yet I felt totally supported and accepted as I am. I felt as though I had found one of my tribes, people I could relate to: these were smart women who were not afraid to bare their souls, for they knew that they would find strength in sharing their vulnerabilities and offering help and support to others. If there's a sisu quality, a way of building resilience that is so essential, it's finding your tribe or tribes.

Time and time again, I have found unexpected solace in seemingly unlikely places—whether it's with people who share a love of cold-water swimming or yoga, talking about how to make the world a better place, sharing ethical values that matter, or being an avid reader or nature lover.

When it comes to loneliness, one of the best quotes that I've come across is by British novelist and journalist Matt Haig, who has written extensively about his struggles with depression on many platforms, including his brilliant book *Reasons to Stay Alive*. In a recent Instagram post, Haig highlighted the fact that loneliness isn't caused by an absence of company—rather, it stems from being with people who aren't on your wavelength and don't understand you.

British-Swiss writer Johann Hari's excellent 2018 book, *Lost Connections: Uncovering the Real Causes of Depression and the Unexpected Solutions*, explores this idea that part of what is ailing people is a lack of true connection.

Hari cites the late John Cacioppo, a professor at the University of Chicago and director of the university's Center for

Cognitive and Social Neuroscience, who found that loneliness isn't the physical absence of other people. It's the feeling that you're not sharing anything that matters with another human being. According to Cacioppo, even if there are people around you such as a spouse, a family, or coworkers in a busy workplace, if you can't share with others the things that matter to you, you'll still feel lonely. And having just one other person who cares and you can share with makes a difference. In his book, Hari also quotes American biologist E. O. Wilson: "People must belong to a tribe."

Finding your tribe—that is, people who value and cherish the same things that you do—is vital.

• • •

ONE MEMBER OF my inspiring and supportive tribe is my dear friend Elina Hirvonen, an incredibly talented writer and filmmaker. She is the first Finnish fiction writer to make the cover of *The New York Times Book Review*, which she did in May 2009 with her brilliantly moving debut novel, *When I Forgot*.

We initially met at a writers' retreat in Iceland some years ago and later developed a deep friendship, sharing ideas and discussing the challenges of juggling a freelance creative career and how easy it is to run out of steam, as it's possible to go 24-7 with all its demands.

Elina and I often have "well-being meets," going for early-morning swims and dips in the cold water at Allas Sea Pool, a public outdoor floating swimming complex in the heart of Helsinki's harbor.

One winter morning while we swam, as the steam rose above the water, re-creating the visual of being in an Icelandic geothermal spa, I asked her about the idea of Finnish humbleness and modesty, and how it relates to the idea of equality.

She shared a lovely anecdote about how she was once interviewing former Finnish prime minister Antti Rinne at an event, and a fan came up to ask for Elina's autograph on a children's book she'd authored, while apologizing to the PM, who completely understood. This, like politicians sharing pasta recipes on social media, seems to me to be a part of the happiness formula, illustrating that there's a nonhierarchical quality to society.

• • •

WHEN IT COMES to connections, finding your own tribe, and the importance of being heard and understood, a friend of mine tells me that one of the loneliest episodes in her life took place after she'd married and had a baby following a whirlwind romance and gradually realized that her new husband was abusive, prone to angry outbursts, and, despite his promises to work, seemed to be frequently teetering on the edge of unemployment and bankruptcy.

But the financial insecurity and his poor mood weren't the worst of it; she wanted to help him and work it out. Rather, it was the challenge of trying to support someone who often took out his anger at the world on her. And that lack of support felt unfair; for example, while she worked overtime to support the family, he would call her repeatedly to inquire when she was coming home to take care of their young child so that he could go out drinking with his friends.

She says the exhausting feeling of having to bear too much of the responsibility was compounded by the double loneliness of having few people to empathize with her because her husband knew how to turn on the charm when he stepped out the door.

• • •

THERE IS SO much of what Lahti said in the Women of Sisu meeting that stays with me, providing solace, especially when I'm feeling weak.

"When you are accepted for who you are—in the moment, authentic and accepted, respected, and seen—then you can let go, and life can dance through you," she noted. She has this touch, this approach of making everyone feel welcome and accepted as they are, which is so incredibly important.

Lahti also speaks to the power of community: "We have all the keys—together," which is so critical. When it seems as if you're on your own, you can feel as though you're not enough—yet there are so many experiences we can all relate to, and when we share them, we feel less alone.

We all have traumas. Some of us are better at hiding them than others, but for many people who are open and honest, we can divide our lives into the time before trauma and the time after trauma. How we deal with that also affects whether we open or close doors for other people. Lahti poses the question: "What do you bring to the room?" Do you want to be a helper, a sympathetic soul who brings light to the world?

"We lean away from suffering, but it's often at those edges that we experience growth," she says. "While there can be a lot of life inside the so-called comfort zone, growth, however, tends to begin at the end of your comfort zone."

Lahti speaks to the importance of having the courage to tell your own story. "I owned the story; this is my story," she says, referring to her own challenges with domestic abuse. "I will not carry someone's shame." And then she asks us, "What's best for you? Don't compare yourself to others. Your warrior's quest—what is it?"

This is something that I often think about, my meaning-of-life quest. And the answer is so clear: It's to help others, to listen to them, to help them feel less alone, to encourage them, and to motivate them, especially when they're feeling low.

Inclusive Sisu

Through our Women of Sisu circle I've met many inspiring women, including Jenni Kallio, who is a special education teacher, author, and PhD student. She is an optimist and enthusiast who believes in people, humanity, compassion, working together, positive psychology, and lifelong learning.

One of her areas of focus is inclusion—that is, preventing exclusion, and developing new approaches to include all children with different needs at school, support their well-being, and help them to meet their potential. Her approach is something we could all benefit from.

Kallio worked as a special education teacher for fifteen years and resided in the United States, Delhi, and Sweden, where she lived from the ages of five to ten.

Understanding and seeing things from many points of view and knowing what it is to be an outsider, especially Kallio's experience of living in Sweden in the 1970s, a time when some Swedes looked down on the Finns as second-class citizens (there is still an inferiority complex that many Finns feel toward Sweden), was in hindsight a sisu-building experience.

She credits that experience of being rootless, yet from so many places, as helping her to build empathy for others. "You identify with the outsider, but you also quickly realize that there's not just one right way to do things," she told me. "And you also understand how important it is to lay those foundations during the early school years, to ensure that no one is left out, that everyone is accepted as they are."

Kallio continued: "Learning the skills needed for life such as psychological capital (self-efficacy, resilience, hope, and optimism), social-emotional learning (SEL), to be oneself, and to be accepted as such are absolutely vital." These are resilience-building skills that are so crucial at a time when children and youth are forming their sense of self.

Equally important is learning to accept and value all kinds of emotions. Listening to and taking guidance from the wisdom of our bodies and accepting all that it is in this moment without judging are keys to compassionate interaction. When we meet one another with appreciation and curiosity rather than judgment, we build psychological safety and open space for learning and growth, says Kallio.

There is a sisu approach that Kallio takes in her work that is essential: challenging the old norms, silos, lack of dialogue, and "this can't be done" attitude with a cooperative mindset. "What matters to you, not what's the matter with you," as she puts it.

Kallio, who is also a neuropsychiatric coach and has a strong belief in the mind-body connection and how it relates to learning and well-being, says that some of the best sessions in which her students learn the most are the ones where they're out in nature, walking and talking. Or just sitting in a circle sharing feelings.

She also speaks strongly in support of social inclusion, which means looking at some of the best practices. In Finland, there is a free school meal system for all students, which means from day care through secondary school, each student receives a warm lunch. Back in 1948, Finland was the first country in the world to start providing a free school lunch to each pupil, with the idea that well-being is built by feeding children a healthy meal not only so that they attend school but also so that they have the energy to learn, and they learn about healthy eating in the process.

While this is beneficial for everyone, it is also a feminist policy, for it is often mothers who are responsible for packing lunches.

A pragmatic approach runs through Kallio's work. "Rather than reprimanding students for missing classes, I tend to say, 'I'm happy to see you, thank you for coming. We missed you in class. What would make coming to school easier for you? Is there anything I can help you with?'"

• • •

FOR MANY, BEING a teacher in Finland is a calling. Interestingly, there are more women teachers than men.

According to 2019 statistics, in Finland at the primary-school level women make up 80 percent of teachers, at junior high 75 percent, and at senior high 60 percent.

When it comes to getting educated, women in Finland are the third most highly educated among OECD countries. According to 2018 statistics, over half of women age twenty-five to sixty-four hold a higher-education degree, and women are completing 59 percent of all university degrees.

Inspired and intrigued by Kallio's pedagogy, I borrowed her 2016 book *Opettamisen Vallankumous: Opettajasta Elinikäisen Oppimisen Valmentajaksi*, from the library. The title roughly translates to "The Teaching Revolution: From Teacher to Lifelong Learning Coach," and the book highlights several lessons from positive psychology.

One of its main tenets is that each person is unique and everyone has, or should have, the possibility to benefit from and utilize their own great potential. As she writes, "Research shows that well-being and quality of life increase when a person has the possibility to exercise and realize their own personal strengths in their daily lives."

She also speaks to the importance of acceptance: "The most important sources of human joy are social situations. According to research, well-being experiences related to social situations and contact with other people are an essential part of a person's well-being and health. Experiencing a connection and a sense of belonging allows one to challenge the limits of one's own abilities and find the courage to transcend them. On the other hand, being left out of the crowd may cause feelings of ineligibility, depression, shame and anger."

She refers to Emilia Elisabet Lahti's wonderful term *arkibriljanssi*, which translates to "everyday brilliance." It means uplifting other people, seeing their potential, and showing appreciation in everyday encounters. It can be as simple as saying thank you to the bus driver, having a happy encounter at the checkout in a grocery store, or smiling at a stranger. Or greeting each student personally every school morning, looking into their eyes, and asking them, "How are you?"

These brief moments stay in our minds and give us confidence, hope, and positive emotional experiences. They shape our brains, broaden our thinking, and improve our cognitive performance. Feedback from other people significantly shapes us, writes Kallio, referencing Lahti's work.

The Courage to Embark on a New Career Later in Life

Though I didn't meet Kaija Suni through the Women of Sisu group, I feel as though she is an honorary member.

Suni is in her fifties and training to be a registered nurse, after a career in communications and the arts, working for 20th Century Fox, Columbia TriStar, and later several galleries. She is a brave soul who has been through much in her personal and professional life and persevered. And she has done what so many people dream of: trained for and started a brand-new career later in life.

She possesses an admirable kind of sisu, a resilience that stops me in my tracks, because she has a beauty, grace, and inner peace that I think so many people spend a lifetime trying to achieve.

As she tells me her life story, that of the overachiever who was a straight-A student and completed an MBA "because that's what you're supposed to do," she also talks about how she worked in the film industry in Finland for more than fifteen years doing marketing and communications, all the while grappling with a slight case of impostor syndrome. "I kept thinking, 'Do I deserve to be here, to go to Cannes, the

Berlin Film Festival, and all of the big American film conventions?'"

At some point, when the teenage horror movie genre became big, Suni started to feel there was a lack of meaning in her work.

Then, alongside work, she completed a BA in art history, which led to work in the field of visual arts. She started working as a freelancer for major Finnish art institutes such as Helsinki's Museum of Contemporary Art Kiasma, which she did for many years, until she felt the work started to dry up.

Suni told me that she took the job too seriously, and then a series of life changes set her on a new path. "In my forties, there was cancer in the form of melanoma on my foot, and breast cancer, the end of a long-term relationship, and then burnout."

She told me that there was also the challenge of juggling a freelance career, and not always having enough work.

But then a surprising thing happened. A life-affirming event, in fact. When Suni was receiving cancer treatments, she was so impressed by how well she was taken care of. The love that she received—she tears up just telling me about it—instilled a strong desire to pay it forward, to give back.

Helping sisu, if you will.

"I think that the fear and despair that I might have felt remained in check because I was so well taken care of and informed about the progress of the treatments," she noted. "I don't think I've ever received such good care in my life as I did during my cancer care. I had this strong feeling that I wanted to do the same for others."

And so she embarked on training for a new career. Suni started studying to be a practical nurse and is now working toward becoming a registered nurse, with the goal of working in youth psychiatric care.

When I asked her about the difference between her previous jet-setting career and her new one, she told me, "I don't need to travel; the journey is here, every day, in the human interactions with the people I meet."

When I asked her about her own sisu, her own resilience, she was humble in a typically Finnish way. She expressed gratitude and said that all the things she'd dealt with and taking on career retraining at a later age were the sum of many things, including living in a country where education and retraining at any age are virtually free. "Plus the fact that I've been able to ask for help and receive it," she added.

In other words, healthy sisu involves not just giving help but also receiving it.

• • •

WHEN I MET Roberta Lima, the Brazilian-Austrian performance artist living in Finland, in the woods on our guided mushrooming tour, she asked me about feminism and sisu, and it set me on a quest.

We arranged to meet up, and Lima, it turns out, lives in Helsinki's Kruunuvuorenranta neighborhood, which is part of the shoreline I see when I swim in the sea.

By water, we're only a few miles apart. But by bicycle and public transit, it's about ten or eleven kilometers (about six miles). As I was having a busy day, I pedaled to the metro station, popped my bike and myself onto the metro, and traveled to the Herttoniemi station, from where it's a relatively short ride of 4.6 kilometers (about three miles) to meet Lima on the shores of Kruunuvuorenranta.

The area has a rich history dating back to the 1500s as a fishing village, and later as a beachfront area, where there were once summer holiday villas in the 1800s and 1900s.

Nowadays, the area is being rapidly developed into a new urban district projected to house about thirteen thousand people by 2030 with architecturally stunning apartment buildings, many of which have spectacular views over the sea to Helsinki's city center.

Over tea, Lima shared her story. She grew up in 1970s dictatorship Brazil, and her father was a military leader. But despite the traditional roles assigned to women in Brazil, she was raised to believe that she could do anything. If her father could lead an army, so, figuratively, could she.

"My dad and I are both soldiers, but we fight very different battles," she said, emphasizing that while she and her father have different ideologies, she was raised with discipline, which she has transformed into resilience.

Lima told me that since moving to Finland several years ago, she'd become fascinated by the concept of sisu. "Sisu is empowering, it's break-through-the-old-stuff, it's forever changing, it's resilience, it's if I don't try, I won't get there. But it's also about not reducing femininity to fragility, it's about standing up for ourselves, nonconformity, speaking out against the collective norm and tapping into resilience, and getting out of the victim mentality," she said.

Speaking from her heart and her art, Lima said much; two significant phrases that stayed with me long after we met were: "It's not our job to make men feel comfortable" and "I won't diminish myself for others."

These, I believe, are the essence of feminist sisu.

Lima also emphasized the role of nature in helping her build fortitude, in her art and in herself. "Finland is good for my body," she said. "My body is connecting to nature, and I'm looking for power, a deeper connection, and support in nature."

Sisu Building

Like many in her field, Finnish resiliency coach Ulrika Björkstam comes to the subject of sisu through a life-changing experience.

In 2008, Björkstam was living and working in Mexico City. On her way home from work one day, she was involved in a terrible accident when a small plane crashed and exploded near her. She suffered severe burns all over her body and face and spent sixteen weeks in the hospital recovering. That was followed by a lengthy sick leave of more than a year. In addition to nearly losing her life, after spending several months in various hospitals in Mexico, the United States, and Finland, she also lost her job and her marriage.

Yet Björkstam speaks to the source of power that allowed her to move on from hopelessness in the midst of a great crisis and find new strength. "A human being will survive if there are no other options," she tells me. "Coping with difficult changes increases resilience and confidence. You are stronger than you think you are."

She quotes Greek philosopher Heracleitus, "The only constant is change," and speaks to how we all experience change, whether from ourselves or from outside, positive or negative.

Despite uncertainty and our fear of the unknown, we have reserves of sisu: "Resilience is within all of us, but in different measures; we don't know how strong we are until our strength is challenged," she says.

She cites a well-known study carried out in Hawaii that followed several hundred people from childhood through adulthood and found that one of the keys to resilience was not that the children didn't experience trauma or difficulty, but that stress can actually build resilience. What made the difference was having at least one understanding person from an early age who believed in that child, encouraging and unconditionally supporting them.

This goes for adults too. Resilience is social—no one survives on their own.

Resilience is social.

Björkstam speaks to resilience and empathy—compassion in action—and says that we're often empathetic toward others and ready to help them, but not always so gentle on ourselves. "What I've come to realize is that people have so much more compassion and understanding toward others but expect (or demand) a lot more from themselves than they would ever do from others. And one of these expectations tends to be that of a quick recovery, to instantly bounce back from adversities. I think it's really important for people to understand that resilience is a process," explains Björkstam.

We spoke about sisu and resilience, which is often thought of as either physical or emotional—but it's not one or the other; neurobiology is connected to how we move, eat, and sleep, says Björkstam. She offered the example of not sleeping well and being too busy to eat a proper lunch, and then at work trying to solve a problem or keep calm when receiving a critical email from a colleague or a client. Self-care through diet, exercise, and rest is important, as our physical wellness affects our emotional resilience—how we are able to regulate our emotions and use our problem-solving skills, for example.

When I asked Björkstam what she thought of in that moment when she found herself on the ground after the accident, she said it wasn't a conscious decision. "I just knew I had to get up, and if I didn't, I wouldn't ever."

But she survived and now thrives.

License to Fail

Though Tomi Kaukinen is not a woman, to me he is a sister of sisu because he has the courage to tell his own honest story about burnout and vulnerability, and to turn cultural expectations upside down. I absolutely adore the fact that "burnout survivor" is part of his LinkedIn profile description, along with his other titles, entrepreneur and keynote speaker.

I'm drawn to Kaukinen's story because he's so vocal about it being okay to not be okay. He speaks to a common narrative that's familiar to so many people. "I'm a guy who has been searching for meaning through performance and doing instead of being, and now I've come home," he told me.

Kaukinen, who grew up in the Swedish capital of Stockholm and is now based in Helsinki, shared his story of how he worked hard, had a successful career, and made a lot of money, but he still wasn't happy.

After studying at the Stockholm School of Economics, he graduated in 2006 and started working for investment banks in fund management. "When I came to my office on the first day of work—apologies to my old bosses, they were lovely—I felt cheated because it was so boring. I thought to myself, 'Is this modern working life?' I was shocked because when I was in school, we had these guys from the business world coming in and telling us that our lives were going to be awesome. And then you realize that the glossy stock photos are just that— glossy stock photos," explained Kaukinen.

He said that the money was a good Band-Aid for a while, and he moved to Finland when he was in his late twenties, thinking that perhaps making more money would make him feel better. Working in real estate fund management, he says, "I had the apartment, the girl, the dog, but every day when I went to the office, I was like 'What, really?' He moved to the start-up world and soon felt the same sense of disenchant-ment.

He started competing in Ironman triathlons to dial up his sense of challenge and achievement. Between chasing money and clients for his company and training for the Ironman, "I was going like a hundred miles an hour on a thirty-mile street all the time," he described.

And then his body stopped him. Unexplained pain led to medical tests, which found nothing physically wrong with him. Kaukinen's psychiatrist said, "I think your brain is trying to stop you."

"I felt this sense of defeat, what a loss, I'm not the über-human that I thought I was, I started to have contempt for myself for being weak, and not being as tough as I thought I was," Kaukinen said. He then made the decision to leave his start-up.

At the age of thirty-eight, he started doing pro bono work for a group in Nigeria. "It was the first time that I felt some meaningfulness," he remembered.

Around the same time, he realized that a lot of people,

especially in working life, feel miserable but don't want or know how to talk about it. So in December 2018 Kaukinen launched Licence to Fail. "James Bond has a license to kill, I have a license to fail. It was such a relief to let the whole facade go and admit that I'd failed, I'd burnt out. I'd spent my whole career being tough and I used to view burnout stories as signs of weakness. But as I came to realize, it's all so fake, especially if you're convinced of your own invincibility," he told me.

Talking openly about failure has been so successful for Kaukinen that he was nominated as Speaker of the Year in Finland in 2020. Speaking out was also therapeutic. "It was the first time in my life that there was no endgame; instead, there was authenticity, being accepted for who I was and am," he said.

"I want everyone to have a license to fail," said Kaukinen. "We would never talk to a friend the way we talk down to ourselves. The world needs more forgiveness—forgive yourself and you might find out that you're like other people. We're all fallible, we all make mistakes, everyone has done something that they're ashamed of—and that's okay."

And that is the heart of healthy, self-accepting sisu.

CHAPTER 7

SISU FOR PLANET EARTH

Eating, Consuming, and Moving for a Better Planet and Better Health

IT'S VERY EASY—AND human—to feel overwhelmed about the state of the planet, as stories about climate change fill our media feeds.

Most of us are aware of the general steps we should be taking to reduce our carbon footprint. But at times it can feel hard to keep up, as there's so much information to take in and stay on top of. We know about recycling, plant-based diets, and avoiding overconsumption.

Like many Finns, my son and I are masters of secondhand finds and have pretty stylish wardrobes (we think) largely comprised of quality thrift store scores and flea market finds. We also endeavor to repair articles of clothing by, for example, sewing up tears or holes, to extend their life cycle.

This Nordic tradition of recycling seems like common sense in these sustainability-focused times. If you can find good-quality pre-loved items—whether clothing or household items—why pay more and buy new? At the same time, it's an *ekoteko*, the Finnish word for a sustainable action.

As secondhand shopping is popular throughout Finland, luckily, there are several reliable flea markets and thrift stores in Helsinki that we frequent, along with excellent local online ones, such as Emmy.fi, that allow you to search for items with a range of filters such as size, color, brand, and style.

Interestingly, one of the activities that Mielenterveystalo.fi, the official public health care sector's mental health digital site, recommends for managing depression, along with a healthy diet, exercise, and spending time with friends, is going to a flea market. It's social, sustainable, and unlikely to break the bank. In other words, you may find the perfect coat or bag or design classic for a very reasonable price without any of the guilt associated with spending lots of money.

Upcycling Sisu

As in other countries, there are many companies in Finland addressing a universal problem and one of the biggest challenges facing the world: how much textile waste ends up in landfills. Globally, an estimated ninety-two million tons of textile waste is created annually.

Several innovative Finnish companies, such as Spinnova, Infinited Fiber Company, and Rester, are providing solutions to the textile waste problem and making international headlines in the process.

Spinnova manufactures wood-based textile fibers completely free of chemicals. Infinited Fiber Company's technology, which turns trash otherwise headed for landfills into a new, premium textile fiber, recently signed a major deal with American clothing company Patagonia. Meanwhile, Rester offers textile recycling solutions to recover business textiles and transform them into a new textile fiber and quality raw material with its end-of-life textile refinement plant, which is reportedly the first of its kind in the Nordics.

There are also many Finnish companies on the clothing front that create new out of old. Globe Hope designs and manufactures ecological products by upcycling discarded materials into clothing, bags, and accessories. Pure Waste produces sustainable fabrics and clothing made up of materials such as offcuts and spinning waste from the clothing and textile industries that would otherwise go to a landfill. And Tauko uses locally sourced industrial textiles that were used in their previous life as bedsheets for hotels and health care to create stylish and practical clothing for women.

• • •

ONE OF THE best ways to exercise some healthy sisu is to reach out to experts for fact-based information, hope, and inspiration. I follow several sustainability groups online, including the Finnish Activist Grannies (called *Aktivistimummot* in Finnish), whose goal is to provide science-based information about climate change and positive examples of what an individual can do to change the world.

For further clarity and expert advice, I reached out to Johanna Kohvakka, an expert in sustainable development and the circular and sharing economy, with a specialty in food waste and plastics. She will also be the head of Helsinki's first recycled shopping mall, where everything from clothing to computers to furniture is repurposed, upcycled, or made out of recycled materials, and therefore is environmentally ethical.

Before moving into a sustainable diet, we start with plastic, which is, of course, so closely linked to what we eat. For example, many people believe that all plastic is bad—not surprising, given the images of floating islands of trash destroying marine life that many have seen.

"Plastic packaging actually plays an important role in preventing food waste, which is a major contributor to climate change," explained Kohvakka, who was also the founder of Finland's first food-waste restaurant, Helsinki-based Restaurant Loop. The eatery, which first opened in 2016, featured changing daily menus based on ingredients, donated by local grocery stores, that are close to their expiration date but still perfectly edible.

Kohvakka is the coauthor of the 2019 Finnish-language book *Hyvä, Paha Muovi* ("Good, Bad Plastic"), which sets out to dispel some of the myths surrounding everyday plastics. "In today's society, packaging is important in order to get products from producer to consumer," she told me. "Plastic packaging also significantly increases the shelf life of many food items and therefore plays a huge role in climate change, as food production accounts for one-third of the environmental burden placed on the planet by human consumption."

According to the Food and Agriculture Organization of the United Nations, roughly one-third of the food produced in the world for human consumption every year—1.3 billion tons—gets lost or wasted. Fruits, vegetables, roots, and tubers have the highest wastage rates of any food. When food is thrown out, the energy, natural resources, and water that

were used to grow it are wasted, as well as the other pro-
cesses associated with it such as manufacturing, transportation, and packaging. Rotting food waste in landfills is a source
of methane, a greenhouse gas that contributes to global
warming.

• • •

CLIMATE ANXIETY IS a mental health issue.

A 2019 report titled *Climate Anxiety*, by Dr. Panu Pihkala, an
adjunct professor of environmental theology at the University
of Helsinki, and published by MIELI Mental Health Finland,
addresses the phenomenon. The study is based on multidisciplinary research and observations made from the practical actions taken to alleviate climate anxiety.

"Climate anxiety is an aspect of the wider phenomenon of
eco-anxiety: it encompasses challenging emotions, experienced, to a significant degree, due to environmental issues
and the threats they pose," writes Pihkala. Essentially, eco-
anxiety impacts our mental health. But it can also activate us
to take action.

"Resilience is often mentioned in this context: the ability
to maintain coping skills while changes take place around us,"
Pihkala notes. Ethical issues and dealing with ambivalence

also significantly affect our ability to remain resilient. But if we take action, we can help alleviate our climate anxiety.

Looking for Solutions

One of the coping skills for climate anxiety is looking for answers. Kohvakka offers an example of good plastic in Finland (these things vary in different countries and regions) that may not seem obvious: "Without plastic wrap, cucumbers would have a shelf life of two to three days and end up in the garbage bin, but with plastic packaging they last two to three weeks."

Another widely held misconception is that some biodegradable plastics are better than regular ones. "Biodegradable plastics can be problematic because they're not accommodated by the current recycling system," says Kohvakka. "They would require their own separate collection system in order to be recycled. As it stands, if biodegradable plastic is recycled with conventional plastic, the entire batch of plastic may be ruined and become unrecyclable."

When it comes to beverages, up to 90 percent of bottles are returned to the bottle return system in Finland. This is owing to a small deposit that provides a monetary incentive, according to Kohvakka's book on plastics, which she coauthored with Liisa Lehtinen, an expert in materials engineering.

According to *Recycling Magazine*, the postconsumer collection rate for plastic PET (polyethylene terephthalate) bottles across Europe is about 63 percent for 2018, though country-by-country collection rates vary from as low as 21 percent in Bulgaria to as high as 96.2 percent in Germany.

Being plastic-savvy and reducing food waste are ways that individuals and restaurants can reduce their impact on the environment, according to Kohvakka. "When it comes to serving beverages and food, moving away from single-use, disposable containers and using reusable ones helps to minimize the environmental impact of our food system," she says.

Kohvakka and Lehtinen started an initiative called Circle-Pack, which has been adopted by several eateries. For those who want takeout, the pair have created—with the help of producers—a series of CirclePack reusable containers that can be purchased against a small deposit.

Throughout Finland, there's a well-established system of lunch restaurants (*lounas ravintolat*) whereby a relatively generous and varied lunch is served for about ten euros (about eleven dollars) that includes several warm mains such as vegan, fish, or meat; a generous salad buffet; bread; coffee; and often dessert. The idea is that everyone should be able to eat a healthy warm meal in the middle of the day either at a restaurant or as takeout as part of their well-being.

• • •

As with domestic households, the less food waste a restaurant produces, the better. With pressure to produce attractive, Instagram-worthy portions to serve diners, getting creative instead of tossing out less-than-perfect-looking fruits and vegetables is vital. It also provides inspiration for households.

The chefs at Restaurant Loop don't know what they'll be making until they step into the kitchen, as items picked up by the food rescue truck vary from day to day. "It's like an episode of *MasterChef* every day," Kohvakka explained in an interview with *The New York Times*. But at Loop they try to make every portion look photogenic so that people will want to share the images online to show what can be made out of ingredients otherwise destined to be wasted.

Most of the food served at Helsinki's Loop is plant-based. "There are many things we can do to lessen our negative impact on the climate, and becoming a vegan and eating seasonal food is one of them," says Kohvakka.

Step by Step

Inspiring others is key when it comes to encouraging everyone to make lifestyle changes, and it's the small sisu steps that make a difference.

For example, rather than trying to instantly cut out all meat (like the daunting task of a crash diet or an extreme fitness regimen), starting out with initiatives such as Meatless Mondays is a good way to proceed.

I liken these incremental efforts to those of learning to adjust expectations after burnout: it's better to try to take a few small steps rather than aiming for perfection and huge changes all at once. Case in point, as studies have shown, catastrophic end-of-the-world scenarios don't encourage people to make changes, hope does.

When I asked Kohvakka what had inspired her climate change work, she replied, "I wanted to do my share of good for the world." She continued, "At some point I started to crave more meaning in my life, going to work every day and you're there for eight, nine hours a day and then what? I started to think that when I'm eighty or ninety years old and I look back, what would I like to see? I had spent ten years working in finance in Frankfurt and Luxembourg and when I realized that that world wasn't giving anything back to me, I resigned from my job."

• • •

KOHVAKKA AND I also spoke about our recycling-consumer lifestyles. "I try not to buy new things anymore," she said. "Through evolution we have developed this feeling that buying something new and owning a lot of stuff gives you security and therefore makes you feel good. I wanted to get past that and question it. Apparently, it came from when we moved from a hunter-gatherer society to an agricultural society, and at that point it was important to gather possessions; for example, how much grain stock you had was important so if there was a poor year you had something to fall back on and your family wouldn't starve." She explained, "I tried consciously to get beyond that and make an effort to buy everything used or pre-owned; for example, even my phone and laptop. Now I feel good when I buy something secondhand, because I know that I'm not using new natural resources."

I shared with her my own frustration, which is that although most of our clothing and furniture and many other things at home are pre-owned, there are some areas of life where secondhand is less of an option, such as technology: my nine-year-old laptop, which has nothing wrong with it in terms of me using it for work, can no longer accept updates because of its age.

Kohvakka understood my frustration, and we spoke about the planned obsolescence of so many things, including broken home appliances such as dishwashers or washing machines, and how sometimes it's impossible to repair them. And they don't always end up being recycled, despite the consumer's best intentions.

"I think the best option would be that the manufacturer would be responsible to the end of a product's life cycle, and take responsibility when the product no longer works and ensure that all of the parts can be recycled," she said.

• • •

KOHVAKKA, WHO HAS spent more time living outside Finland than in one place in the country, considers herself rootless, but says that she really likes being in Finland now because when it comes to climate change, it's so easy to find like-minded people who are addressing the same issues—one's own tribe, so to speak. "I feel like Helsinki is a climate change leader, as there are so many people who are so aware and on the same page," she says.

That eco-awareness can be as simple as knowing to look

critically beyond greenwashing. "It's important to be aware of the facts because there can be, for example, napkins that are dyed brown so they appear more ecological. This leads people to think that they are doing an *ekoteko*—that is, something ecological—when in fact that's not the case," Kohvakka says. Another example is the false labeling of products as biodegradable or natural.

Kohvakka also enlightens me on the simple daily actions that make a difference. For example, in Finland, people eat a lot of rye and other bread. Previously, I never thought twice about tossing a piece of stale or moldy bread into the biodegradable waste, even thinking that I was doing a good turn as it would change into soil.

But it turns out that's not the case. "The environmental impact of one piece of bread is larger than the plastic bag that it's packed into, because of the emissions that it has already generated and the amount of energy needed to recycle it," says Kohvakka, who was also instrumental in a pilot program in Helsinki that trained advisers to help with recycling issues, optimizing home waste management solutions, and providing tips and inspiration for a zero-waste lifestyle, along with resources for reduction, sorting, and recycling.

The Future of Food

There are a lot of initiatives around the world to address the issue of food waste.

In Finland, one such initiative is ResQ Club, which connects sustainable restaurants, cafés, and grocery shops with consumers via an app that allows people to use location-based mobile and web services to purchase food at a discounted rate that would otherwise be thrown out. The idea is that consumers can "rescue surplus food in their proximity."

We can shape the world we live in with each bite we take. A sisu-fueled diet is one that makes a positive difference to the planet by preferring a plant-based lifestyle comprising seasonal and local foods.

There is a long tradition of foraging in Finland, for berries, mushrooms, and herbs that are packed with nutrition and free. But when it comes to the bigger global picture, not everyone has the option of foraging or growing their own food wherever they may live; bigger sisu solutions are needed.

Many companies in Finland have brought practical options to the market, ranging from fava bean innovator Beanit, which bills itself as "the world's first plant-based protein product made from Nordic Fava beans," to oat innovators Gold&Green,

which brings together a combination of Nordic oats and legumes.

Sisu Gold

Food solution innovator Solar Foods, a Finnish start-up founded in 2017 by former scientists from the VTT Technical Research Centre of Finland, the national research institute, has created a protein from air using carbon-capture technology, which is sisu gold. This is because their nonagricultural, carbon-neutral protein, which looks a bit like saffron, could provide a solution to global hunger and address the issue of agricultural drain.

I met two of the cofounders of Solar Foods, Pasi Vainikka and Juha-Pekka Pitkänen, at their secret lab housed in a nondescript garage on the outskirts of Helsinki. As I donned the mandatory white lab coat, I felt as though I'd gone back to Science 101. In their spotless lab, there was a bubbling silver-colored bioreactor with a series of tubes going in and out, a fermenter, and several other very scientific-looking pieces of equipment.

In a nutshell, Solar Foods' Solein protein is made by growing a microbe in liquid in a fermentation tank. It's like the process used in breweries, but instead, Solar Foods' microbe uses water, carbon-dioxide capture, and renewable electricity to make protein, a food source.

Essentially, Solein is "food out of thin air." While that's their official slogan, it really does sum up the process. And all of it is powered by renewable energy, minimizing the product's carbon footprint. Standing in their lab, I felt a sense of awe.

"In order to save the planet from climate change, we need to disconnect food production from agriculture," Vainikka told me.

The challenge with agriculture is that it takes up so many of our natural resources—more than we can spare, in fact. "As a protein source, Solein's comparative greenhouse gas emissions are approximately one percent that of meat protein and about twenty percent of plant protein production," explained Pitkänen. "The sustainability impact of Solein goes even further. Changing the way protein is produced will have an effect not only on greenhouse gases but also on changes in land use, soil impoverishment, biodiversity, and the status of water systems."

The idea, according to the cofounders, is that in the future, food can be produced in extreme conditions such as the desert, in the Arctic, or even in space. "We want to be the world's first commercial facility to produce food by using carbon dioxide and electricity as raw materials. We want to disconnect food production from the accelerating consumption on natural resources," Vainikka said. This would mean alleviating a major burden on ecosystems in Finland and the world.

The cofounders possess a typical Finnish humbleness. As we stood in our white lab coats, they were soft-spoken about their mission, which is to "save at least one planet."

As Vainikka explained, Solein is a novel food, a natural source of protein that is flavorless and can be added to smoothies and sauces alike. It is full of nutrients, including vitamin A, iron, and B vitamins, and not high in carbohydrates, which addresses another problem: undernourishment and the lack of vitamins in many people's diets. When it comes to cost, they point out it's cheaper than red meat, which means it has the potential to provide a carbon sink solution on a massive scale.

How much has the cofounders' Finnish upbringing influenced their creation? They point out that they grew up with an awareness of overconsumption and its effects on the planet. Vainikka also credits the nonhierarchical Finnish academia and research scene. "Whether it's in the sauna or in academic or tech circles, you can take your ideas forward without having to deal with hierarchy. That makes a really big difference, especially when you're in the initial stages with an idea you want to take forward and find support for with people who take you seriously and accept you equally," he observed.

Solar Foods recently received €10 million (about $12 million) from the Finnish Climate Fund, which will allow it to start commercial-scale production of Solein so that its industrial facility in Finland will be fully operational by 2023.

This is a consumer food evolution, based on a sisu organism that comes from Finnish nature. "There's a lot of sisu in the cell," says Pitkänen, adding, "This is environmental gold."

English journalist George Monbiot, known for his political and environmental journalism, has been quoted in a feature by the BBC as saying that although he's generally pessimistic about the future of the planet, Solar Foods has given him hope. He is not alone.

Pedal Power

Turning from food to movement, when it comes to getting around, private transport is one of the biggest sources of greenhouses gases.

My son and I are very lucky to live in an apartment in central Helsinki, which means that we can cycle or walk just about everywhere, which is often faster and easier than any other option. If our journey is longer, we can use the well-functioning and safe public transit system.

In many cities around the world, it's simply not an option to be carless. There are a number of reasons for this, including long distances that need to be covered daily that are not viable or safe without a car. For example, in L.A. driving a car versus taking public transit can mean the difference between a fifteen-minute drive and a two-and-a-half-hour commute.

In Helsinki, we can easily get around by bicycle, with the added bonus of a free workout and some fresh air. We see our neighbors and participate in the world. I've had far more interesting social encounters on my bike than in an automobile.

We also don't have to spend time looking for parking, or paying for all the maintenance and other costs a car requires, which frees up our resources.

I would rather use the time to pedal or walk outdoors (small sisu-building activities)—yes, whatever the weather—or occasionally take a tram or public transit than spend time and money on a car.

• • •

HELSINKI HAS THE ambitious goal of being the world's most functional city and becoming carbon neutral by 2035. The promotion of cycling and integrating it as a functional part of the transport system is key.

According to Helsinki's Bicycle Action Plan 2020–2025,

"Cycling is promoted because it helps achieve time savings, more efficient use of space, health benefits, environmental benefits, financial benefits and improved traffic safety. The promotion of cycling is not an end in itself; rather, it is a tool for creating a safer, more comfortable and more functional urban environment."

I met Helsinki's cycling coordinator, Oskari Kaupinmäki, outside Oodi, which is the city's main library, an architectural wonder in the heart of the city and an ode to a love of books and reading.

Finland is one of the world's most literate countries, with a literacy rate of about 99 percent. It's also a bookworm nation. A few years ago, when Finnish NHL hockey player Kevin Lankinen mentioned that one of his favorite books was *A Little Life* by American writer Hanya Yanagihara, sales of the Finnish-language edition of the book skyrocketed in Finland and it quickly sold out.

Incidentally, the Finnish library system is unbelievably well stocked, offering virtually all the latest fiction and nonfiction English-language titles, despite the country's official languages being Finnish and Swedish.

Since opening in 2018, Oodi has become the city's living room. More than just a place to borrow or read a book, it's where locals gather, have a cup of coffee or wine, borrow a sewing machine, or use a 3D printer or one of the games rooms. Its unisex bathrooms speak to equality.

It also speaks to the country's design heritage. Architecturally stunning with a combination of glass and steel and wood, Oodi is also an energy-efficient building.

Kaupinmäki and I met outside the library, which is located on Kanslaistori, one of the city's main squares. As we sat on the benches outside, Kaupinmäki told me that he became so passionate about cycling as a mode of transport because as a preteen and teenager, he spent several years living in Canada's Sudbury, known as a mining town. "Having grown up in Finland, where we had the freedom to ride our bikes just about everywhere, living in Sudbury I felt a sense of irritation and realized how little freedom teenagers had. Before we got our driver's licenses the only means of getting around was by car and we were dependent on being driven everywhere by our parents," he recalled.

He told me that he vividly remembers the absurdity of being at a friend's house in Canada and wanting to leave to go home, but walking the relatively short distance seemed an unviable option to his friend's parents. Experiences like that led him to his current career path as an urban traffic planner. "As I've gained more experience, I've found that promoting sustainable transportation has become a topic of high interest, especially when it comes to cycling and the idea of a human-scaled city," he said.

One of the things that stood out in our conversation is a recent paradigm shift, which is the understanding that it's necessary and far more conducive to work together to incorporate all forms of transport and avoid a car-versus-bicycle mentality.

Kaupinmäki says the paradigm shift involved considering cycling more as an integral part of the transportation system rather than a marginalized mode that is given space only when it's available and not given, for example, to cars.

It also means that cycling is a form of transport, not merely a hobby, and requires facilities throughout the city, such as public bicycle pump machines at metro stations and covered parking.

Another reality is that a lot of people will choose to ride a bike if it offers the fastest and easiest option to get from A to B, not necessarily because of sustainability concerns. In Helsinki, if the journey is between one and five kilometers (up to about three miles), pedaling is often the fastest solution.

Cycling also adds to the city's vibrancy, as people on two wheels can stop and chat with friends or pop into a café or shop, while generally taking care of their well-being. It's a social event.

I think of the late Bill Cunningham, the legendary fashion photographer who whipped around New York on a bicycle until he was in his eighties: Would he have gotten as many great shots if he'd not been cycling?

• • •

THE CITY'S GOAL is to raise the bicycling share from 11 percent to 20 percent by 2035, according to Kaupinmäki. This is part of its plan to be carbon neutral by 2035. In Helsinki, there are 130 kilometers (about 80 miles) of dedicated bike lanes. The goal is for all the bike paths to be suitable for everyone, from eight- to eighty-year-olds.

Kaupinmäki says he's been very inspired by Copenhagen's model. In the Danish capital, of all trips made to, from, and in the city, 28 percent were made by bicycle in 2018. About 50 percent of trips made by Copenhageners within the city were made on two wheels, which Kaupinmäki says is astounding.

He emphasized that Helsinki's main goal is a multidisciplinary holistic approach to integrating all the transportation systems: bicycle, walking, public transport, and, yes, the car.

And because many of the bicycle paths in Helsinki are well maintained during the snowy and icy winter months by means of salt brushing, which means they're snow- and ice-free, it's a safe way to get around.

When it comes to resilience, Kaupinmäki raises an important point: "Part of the idea of mobility is to teach kids, for example, to be more active by walking and cycling to where they need to go, not, for example, getting used to being chauffeured by car to sports and other activities by their parents." In a safe country like Finland, where it's not uncommon for kids as young as eight or nine to cycle, walk, or take public transit on their own, this is a good example of sisu-building.

Extreme cold weather is not an obstacle to cycling in Finnish cities, even northern ones such as Oulu (known as the winter-cycling capital of the world) or the eastern city of Joensuu. A national government scheme called Finnish Schools on the Move aims to find ways to keep children more active, including by encouraging them to walk or cycle to school.

The health benefits of exercise for people of all ages are massive, especially for older people, as it can help reduce the risk of dementia, type 2 diabetes, some types of cancer, depression, heart disease, and more.

Functional Cities Increase Well-Being

"We want to be the most functional city in the world," Kaupinmäki told me. And part of that is the cycling-friendly equation.

It's also a health care event, as cycling has a positive effect on people's well-being because it boosts their health and helps cut the costs of health care. There are numerous health bene-fits to regular cycling, including increased cardiovascular fit-ness, muscle strength, and flexibility; improved posture and coordination; and decreased stress levels.

This is sisu in action—building resilience and strength into daily life, one car-free ride at a time.

CHAPTER 8

SOWING THE SISU SEEDS
OF THE FUTURE

O N A RECENT spring morning I took the train from Helsinki to Ii, a community of about ten thousand people in northern Finland, about 640 kilometers (just under 400 miles) from Helsinki.

When I left Helsinki at just past six in the morning, it was about 10 degrees Celsius (about 50 degrees Fahrenheit), but by the time I reached Oulu, Finland's fourth-largest city, located near the Arctic Circle, snowflakes were falling.

As my mission was related to sustainability and the environment—Ii has the ambitious goal of being the world's first zero-waste community—I decided to take the train and a bus rather than fly. After the six-hour train ride, I hopped on a bus and headed to Ii, which is pronounced "ee" (in Finnish the letter *i* sounds like *e* in English).

In Ii I met Johanna Jakku-Hiivala, my host, for the visit. She works for Micropolis, which accelerates green and sustainable growth in northern Finland. I also met her friend Heidi Takalo, an engineer, who had come along in part because she's a winter swimmer, and I'd requested that before we get down to work and get acquainted with Ii, we go for a cold-water swim.

This is an intentional icebreaking (pun intended) technique that I've employed in many places, partly because I've never met an unfriendly winter or cold-water swimmer, and partly because a visit to an area's cold watering hole is a great way to get to know the locals.

We went for a refreshing dip off the dock at Vihkosaari in the Ii River, where the water is about 5 or 6 degrees Celsius (about 40 degrees Fahrenheit), while on the nearby sandy beach, a group of schoolchildren were enjoying an afternoon picnic—even though it was about 2 degrees Celsius (about 35 degrees Fahrenheit) outside—with a few cartwheels and a game of tag. Being outside in the fresh weather didn't seem to bother them one bit.

In true Finnish style, after a few icy dips, we headed for a sauna, which is such a quintessentially cultural thing to do in the country, where there are an estimated 3.3 million saunas for a population of 5.5 million people.

Having a sauna together is perhaps the cultural equivalent in other countries of having a few drinks, breaking the ice by chatting in the sauna, where everything is stripped away—quite literally. For as you sit, naked (you can wrap yourself in a towel if it's too much) in the hot steam, it doesn't matter what your job title is, how much you own or earn, or anything else, for that matter. The sauna is a great equalizer, where little else matters other than the conversation and courtesy toward your fellow sauna-goers.

The sauna is a great equalizer.

This is the Finnish temple of relaxation and calm, where each ladle of water thrown over the hot rocks brings *löyly*, a relaxing hot steam that cleanses both mind and body as you sweat out the toxins and find a relaxed sense of calm—Finnish happiness, if you will.

Nudity, especially when it comes to the sauna, is not a big deal in Finland. And though initially, when I moved there, I found it a bit awkward, as I grew accustomed to it, I found liberation in it. For it's not about you. No one is particularly concerned about how you look, and you quickly come to realize that bodies come in all shapes and sizes and that's perfectly normal.

• • •

Johanna, Heidi, and I spoke about everything from body image to the challenges of everyday life. As we sat in the sauna, we were equals. And this is something that ties into the whole happiness concept—when people ask why Finland is ranked the happiest country on Earth, I think they are often surprised by the simple answers.

In Finland, people spend a lot of time in nature, practice activities such as cold-water swimming, relax and reset in the sauna, and enjoy simple activities that are accessible to all, such as foraging for berries or mushrooms in the forest.

I recounted how a French journalist asked me questions about the sauna and this idea of equality in nudity, which seemed foreign to her and something that she was trying to grasp.

"Could you go for a sauna with Prime Minister Sanna Marin?" the French journalist asked, somewhat apprehensively. I replied that yes, I could, but that likely the PM was so busy that there wasn't time for public saunas in her schedule.

Part of the Finnish mindset is that if Marin and I were in the same public sauna, general sauna etiquette is such that though I might acknowledge her presence with a greeting, as she is a well-known figure, I would respect her privacy and her sauna time and leave her be.

After a good steam, Johanna, Heidi, and I laughed so hard over our shared evening meal that our cheeks became flushed. We were in such good spirits as we shared the collective challenges of coming out of the pandemic—Wait, I can't wear sweatpants all day anymore?—and commiserated about how trying to be sustainable sometimes feels like a full-time job. Which is why the next day's program brought a breath of relief.

• • •

EARLY THE FOLLOWING morning, Johanna took me to meet the mayor of Ii, Ari Alatossava, at his home in the charming historic Hamina area, which dates back to the fourteenth century and is among Finland's oldest trading posts.

En route, as if on cue, against the backdrop of falling snowflakes and the photogenic wooden houses in shades of green, yellow, and red, a woman walking her dog was picking up garbage. This, Johanna told me, is one of the many citizen-led initiatives in the community to tackle climate change.

When we arrive at our destination, several friendly dogs scampered into the foyer of the house as we stepped inside from the cold. Alatossava greeted us with a warm smile and welcomed us into his kitchen, where on the counter lay a fresh tray of triangle-shaped tea biscuits that he'd baked for us, which he later served to us with sencha tea in mugs emblazoned with the beloved and popular Moomin characters, a national treasure, first created by Swedish-speaking Finnish artist Tove Jansson back in the 1940s in a series of books and comic strips.

For the record, I've interviewed politicians over the years and usually it's involved a visit to an official office and going through a fairly intensive security check, among other things. This was the first time I'd been invited into a politician's home and been served homemade baked goods.

The laid-back quality of our visit speaks to the humbleness that I've experienced in so many places in Finland, which is part of the happiness formula. You are accepted as you are, as a person, as an equal. This is remarkably refreshing and authentic, especially as I've lived in places such as England where your class, your accent, everything matters and puts you in a category as soon as you've opened your mouth.

Ii's ambitious sustainability plan was captured in a viral BBC news clip called "Finland's New Generation of Climate Heroes" that features a two-minute trailer for a documentary about what people in the small northern town are doing to curb climate change and achieve their zero-waste goal by 2050.

Alatossava says that sustainable development has always

interested him. The question that has long held his interest is: How can a small community make a difference? "It doesn't need to be rocket science. In Ii, early on we realized that some of it was very basic—for example, let's invest in local geothermal, solar, and wind energy to keep the profits here rather than paying a large corporation for heating costs with the profits going outside of our community," he explained.

Ii stopped using fossil fuels and is rapidly reducing carbon emissions. Their target, which they've already reached, was to reduce carbon emissions by 2020, thirty years ahead of the European Union (EU) target.

One of their events, Climate Arena, the first national climate festival, held in 2019, is based on the idea that finding solutions to climate change requires everyone's participation, from political leaders to those in business, science, and the arts to citizens and residents.

A lot of the solutions that Ii has employed are based on old-fashioned common sense. For example, when it comes to grocery shopping, it can be as simple as supporting your local independent store. If you're not a patron and you'd rather drive to a superstore or a big-box store farther away so that you can, save ten or twenty cents on a product, it's worth considering how much you are really saving when you factor in the time and fuel spent driving to the store.

"The world is crying out for sustainability solutions," Alatossava told me. "If a small community in northern Finland can do things to make a difference, everyone and anyone can. It doesn't need to be big, or expensive, or even systemic."

Climate Heroes

"Resource wisdom" is one of Ii's practical yet brilliant ways of effecting change. It refers to the children and youth of Ii, who have become international climate heroes because of the strong traditions of climate education in the community, as well as because of their actions.

An important incentive has been the 50/50 model. Essentially, this is a climate solution whereby students save electricity, water, and heating usage through their actions and then receive half of the money saved to buy things such as sports equipment for their schools.

Alatossava told me, "Even if we achieve something, it's no reason to stop," which strikes me as such a sisu comment—you don't stop, you continue moving forward.

And that's the attitude that makes the difference.

Ii's achievements to date include: In ten years carbon dioxide emissions have been reduced by 62 percent. There are no oil-heated properties; all municipal buildings are heated using renewable energy. The municipality uses ten times more solar power than any other Finnish municipality (the average share of solar power in Finnish electricity generation is 0.2 percent) and all municipal employees drive electric cars.

• • •

OUR NEXT STOP was the local secondary school to chat with a few teenagers about how to make an eco-difference.

We met with three young women between the ages of fifteen and seventeen—Helmi, Nea, and Hanna—to chat about sustainability, as in this community a lot of the impetus and sustainability initiatives have come from the youth.

As they spoke, I was impressed not only by their knowledge, but by their Nordic confidence. The teens were not overly self-promotional, but they had substance in that they knew what they were talking about, yet were diplomatic and humble in their delivery.

When I asked them why sustainability is important, Helmi told me, "We have to act because we have the power to do so and it's important in order to ensure the best possible future."

Their examples of their own sustainability actions were straightforward yet powerful. Nea replied, "I bike to school and home every day." Helmi said, "We make sure that we turn off the lights when we leave a classroom, and we recycle and compost." She added, "We're fortunate because we have free school food."

I find this incredibly insightful, as a lot of schoolchildren in Finland complain about school food because what's on offer is not always their favorite meal. I'm not sure that many schoolchildren here realize how fortunate they are, for there are so many countries around the world where pupils are not fed during the day.

Another eco-step they take at the school is lowering the temperature by a few degrees in order to reduce heating energy, which means the need to wear an extra-warm sweater sometimes.

"It can be a bit chilly," admitted Hanna.

"Small actions matter."

When I asked about the future, they were optimistic and philosophical. Helmi said, "Small actions matter."

I asked her if there were some best practices she'd like to share with the world, and she said that the bottle recycling system in Finland is pretty cool. "It encourages people not to litter with plastic bottles."

In Finland, 460 million plastic bottles are returned every year. Finland is one of the world's leaders in recycling beverage containers, thanks to Palpa, a nonprofit management company. The return system is based on a deposit, a fee that is refunded to the consumer when they return a bottle or a can. The recycling rate of aluminum cans is 96 percent, and more than 90 percent of bottles and cans end up being recycled, according to statistics.

Other positive sustainable actions include moving toward a more plant-based diet, which is healthier for ourselves and the planet.

When I asked the girls about their future dreams, Helmi replied, "My dream is to do something positive, to have an impact and to curb climate change."

That neatly sums up the sisu sustainability ideal. Each of us—regardless of our age and circumstances—has more inner strength than we might imagine. It's this inner strength and resolve that can power us through tough times—and change our world for the better.

CHAPTER 9

TEN PRACTICES FOR EVERYDAY SISU

Strength-Building Habits

WHEN I WAS at one of my lowest and weakest points, I picked up a pen and wrote down several sisu to-do goals in my notebook.

It was a simple list:

Sit in a café with my son and drink a cup of coffee while
   enjoying his company.
Swim in the sea and have a sauna.
Walk in the woods with a friend without getting winded.
Read a book.
Be able to do a few push-ups and sit-ups again.
Get a pedicure and wear sandals.

Put on a summer dress.

Have friends over for tea.

Write something that matters and helps other people.

Go toward the light, toward people who encourage,
    support, and build up others.

That list was followed by the names of the people who needed me to get well: my son, family and friends, colleagues, and others who depended on me. A gentle self-reminder was also included: in order to take care of others, I needed to take care of myself.

In hindsight, that list seems almost banal, comprising very regular, easy activities. Yet at the time it was written, it represented a list of personal challenges.

Whatever challenges you're facing, accepting yourself and your vulnerabilities and figuring out how to deal with them and move forward—albeit slowly—without giving up is the key to healthy sisu.

Consider a baby's first steps. An infant doesn't just start walking one day. First, they practice by pulling themselves up to stand using a piece of furniture or a person as a helpful prop. Then, as they gradually become stronger and gain confidence, they progress to a few wobbly solo stands and those first few shaky steps. As they start to navigate the world on foot, there are many falls along the way.

Whenever I feel as though I'm not moving quickly enough, I remind myself that small steps are often much more effective in achieving a goal than an all-or-nothing approach. The first time I tried winter swimming, my icy dip lasted barely five seconds before I scrambled back up the ladder to the dock from the shock. It took months of cold-water immersion and acclimatization before I was able to do a few breaststrokes in the sea.

In order to strengthen our sense of sisu, whatever our situation, we need to find the activities and actions that help us become stronger.

A healthy sisu mindset is a can-do, will-try, courageous, not-afraid-of-failing approach to life that's nurtured and strengthened by habits and practices, many of which are best practiced daily.

1 Mind-Body Sisu

Taking care of your mental and physical well-being is absolutely key to improving your fortitude.

As we know—and there is much science to back it up—physical and mental health are inextricably linked. When you feel physically poorly, it will very likely impact your mood, and when you feel mentally weak, it will very likely impact your physical well-being.

Which is why it's important to incorporate movement into your day and find a form of activity that you enjoy doing. Whether it's gentle stretches, a short stroll, getting up from your desk to walk around, dancing, or a hard-core gym workout, moving your body can literally help to change your mind.

While a strong body can facilitate a strong mind, it's important to note that everybody has their own definition of strength. Simply put, fitness means having a body that's comfortable to live in, that works for you and allows you to take care of your regular daily life and maybe even challenge yourself.

This may seem obvious, but when it comes to exercise it's important to find activities that you enjoy and that work with your budget and schedule. It's very difficult to make a regular habit out of a physical activity you dislike. Other, equally important considerations include access, time, and cost. Most of us have budgets, which is why keeping it simple and sensible makes sense. If you need to travel great distances, invest in expensive equipment, or pay large fees, it will likely make it more difficult to sustain and maintain a practice. That's part of the reason why activities such as walking and jogging are so popular, because they can be done just about anywhere at any time and they're pretty much free.

An excellent sisu hack is the Finnish concept of *arkiliikunta,* or everyday exercise, which means benefiting from incidental exercise. For example, walking or biking to work, to the grocery shop, or to a café to meet friends instead of driving there are excellent examples. When you make *arkiliikunta* a regular habit, you may find that on the days you skip it you feel less energetic and crave it.

Simple activities such as walking and cycling also have myriad health benefits, from getting your heart rate up to offering many of the muscles in your body a mini-workout and boosting your mood.

2 Mental Health Maintenance Sisu

Just about everyone struggles with their emotions from time to time, some people more than others.

When you bottle up or dismiss your feelings and don't deal with them, they can come out in unexpected ways. The simple act of talking about what's on your mind with someone—whether a professional or a trusted friend—can improve your mood and make you feel better.

When you deal with your own issues, it's not only good for you, but it can also help others so that you don't inadvertently take out your own unresolved traumas on them. This can increase your self-awareness, which helps to build a stronger sense of sisu.

3 Empathetic Sisu

Compassion for others means trying to look at things from other perspectives and points of view. Having empathy for other people also means respecting them and their choices and not assuming that our own perspectives and experiences are universal.

We can also benefit from showing ourselves some empathy in the form of self-compassion. We often talk to ourselves in ways that we wouldn't dream of speaking to our dearest friends. Like bullies, we can belittle and berate ourselves.

Self-compassion means accepting and respecting our own strengths and weaknesses. It means giving ourselves a break, understanding that even when things don't go according to plan, we've tried our hardest and that's fine and we can try again tomorrow.

Compassion can also be about recognizing that when someone treats you poorly, it's likely not personal. Sure, it may be upsetting, but you can try to conserve your energy and save yourself some grief by realizing that mean people are often acting out of their own interests, fears, or unresolved issues. It's actually more about them than it is about you.

Self-compassion also means embracing your vulnerabilities. It doesn't mean that you need to share all your traumas and quirks with everyone, but seeking support and being open can often lead to surprising results. For example, admitting that you suffer from depression may lead other people to share their experiences and struggles, and together, you will both feel less alone.

4 Self-Care Sisu

In our busy, always-on, 24-7 lives, it's easy to neglect the basics of taking care of ourselves, such as eating properly and getting enough rest. It's hard to build up your strength if you're running on empty and exhausted.

So, in addition to eating a balanced diet, getting enough rest doesn't just mean taking short breaks during the workday, it also means practicing good sleep hygiene (putting digital devices away) and ensuring that you get a proper night's sleep. As with many things, self-care is a continual process: one well-slept night doesn't fix months of sleep deprivation. If there's an ongoing issue with insomnia, it's good to look into it and try to find out the root cause in order to get help.

Self-care sisu also means learning to say no and recognizing what works best for you. Some people thrive in crowds and with constant company, while others need doses of quiet, reflective alone time. Recognizing your own needs is part of the key to building up resilience.

5 Sauna Sisu

Another truly Finnish hack for boosting your sisu is taking that quintessential Finnish steam bath, the sauna, for its many health benefits. In addition to providing a soothing experience for mind and body as you sweat out toxins and stresses, this gadget-free zone is *the* place for taking a wellness break.

It also provides a good exercise in challenging yourself,

because remember, if you sample a sauna in Finland, the proper way to enjoy a good steam is naked. However, men and women sauna separately, and if you feel uncomfortable with being nude, you can always wrap a towel around yourself.

The sauna experience offers good practice in tapping into your sisu and getting over yourself, especially if you come from a culture where nudity is a big deal. The focus in the Finnish sauna is not on *me* but rather on *we*, and it can be very liberating to realize that no one cares how you look without your clothes on and that bodies come in all shapes and sizes— and that's natural and normal.

6 Connect with Nature Sisu

The Finnish way of life is intricately connected to nature. Whether by spending time in parks, forests, or near (or in) lakes or the sea, being in nature helps us to rejuvenate and rebuild our depleted energy reserves.

Activities such as hiking, skiing, swimming, and foraging help our brains and our bodies find balance, but they also help us to see the bigger picture and return to our roots.

7 Sustainability Sisu

A good sense of sisu means making sustainable choices that help not hinder, life on planet Earth. That means taking action and making green choices in the ways we move and eat and how we consume.

On an individual level that means moving toward a more plant-based diet, reconsidering consumption habits—can you buy secondhand or rent or borrow?—recycling everything possible, and, making greener transportation choices, for example.

Here are a few challenges to think about: Would you consider investing in a few long-lasting, quality pieces of clothing over a large quantity of fast fashion that presents a recycling challenge? Can you carry a reusable bottle for water or a travel mug rather than using single-use or plastic options? Can you try to eliminate food waste by cooking creatively and not loading up your plate with more food than you can eat?

8 Pragmatic Sisu

One of the simplest ways to build up strength is to realistically try to anticipate situations.

An obvious example is that if your physical strength often wanes when you get hungry, get into the habit of carrying a bottle of water and a snack in your bag or knapsack, especially if you know that there may not be a grocery store or café nearby.

The same skill of planning ahead can also be applied to maintaining your psychological strength and energy. Limit the amount of time you spend with people who suck the sisu out of you. That includes those whose criticism is often destructive rather than constructive and those who have a habit of turning something simple into a complicated endeavor. Favor those who support others, lift you up, and leave you feeling like anything is possible, because they're looking to address problems and challenges with potential solutions.

9 Take a Sisu Pause

When life or a situation seems overwhelming, learn to take a pause when possible. Some things need to be dealt with immediately, but a great many can be handled with a diplomatic "Thank you, I'll think it over and get back to you as soon as possible."

That means, especially if you're overwhelmed or unsure

about what to do, you can gather your thoughts, perhaps do a bit of research on the best plan of action, and instead of acting in the heat of the moment, have a good think.

Give yourself permission to stop, take a few deep breaths, and, if possible, walk (indoors works; outdoors is even better) while you think about what needs to be done and sort out your thoughts. Whether it's a short pause or a longer one, a bit of reflection and time can go a long way.

10   Sisu Energy Management

Learn to manage your energy so that you can do the things that sustain and nourish you. Knowing when you need to ask for help is a sign of resilience and a way to practice good personal energy management.

Try to read around, stay informed, and listen to different points of view.

Readjust preconceived notions and embrace the elements. While winter swimming is an excellent example of sisu for its range of benefits, it's also a good example of turning what may seem like a challenge into an asset. Instead of sitting around and complaining about the weather and daydreaming about being on a warm beach, winter swimming is about taking your circumstances and turning them around to make them work to your advantage. Winter cyclists share a joke about cycling through sleet: it's like a free facial.

Sisu it up.

EPILOGUE

O N A WARM day in early spring, I walk across Helsinki's iconic and popular tourist destination Senate Square on my way to the National Library of Finland.

On the northern side of the square, the grand cathedral, Tuomiokirkko, called the Helsinki Cathedral in English (although a literal translation would be the "Church of Judgment"), reflects the stronghold of Lutheranism as the state religion in Finland. Of the country's 5.5 million population, 3.7 million belong to the Lutheran church.

The neoclassical white cathedral, one of the world's largest Lutheran churches, dates back to 1852 and features sculptures of the twelve apostles that guard the city, making its rooftop collection one of the world's largest of zinc sculptures.

Surrounding it on the square are grand university and governmental buildings in rich shades of yellow that were designed by Carl Ludvig Engel, the same architect who designed the Lapinlahden Lähde community center, where Visit Peace is located.

As I cross the street and approach the National Library of Finland, also designed by Engel, I feel a sense of awe, for this is one of the most renowned landmarks and public libraries of early nineteenth-century Empire architecture.

Inside, there are motifs from classicism and references to the ancient world. The symmetrical layout of the library halls harks back to the bathhouses of the Roman emperor Diocletian. This place is like a spa for the mind.

This is also the oldest and largest scholarly library in Finland. It's responsible for the collection and preservation of the country's published national heritage.

I've come to see the first comprehensive dictionary of the Finnish language, which dates back to 1745 and was written by bishop and professor Daniel Juslenius. It features the first mention of the word *sisu*, in the form of *sisucunda*, a location in the human body where strong emotions can be felt.

In our ever-online world, experiencing this work in person is a rarity.

Getting here required some serious sisu. After several false starts and dozens of emails, it turned out that during the pandemic, only those with a library card could apply for special access to materials such as Juslenius's dictionary. Yet applications for new library cards were granted only in person, which was not possible due to the pandemic. Which meant that as I didn't have a card to this special library, it wasn't possible to apply for one.

After much back-and-forth, I spotted an Instagram update saying that the National Library had changed its policy and given the circumstances would be granting new library cards via online applications.

I immediately put together my application. Happily, I received an email a few days later saying the application had been approved.

• • •

AFTER I SIGN in and store my knapsack and coat in the cloakroom, I step into the magnificent main hall of the library, with its high book-lined room and windowed cupola that allows light to stream in.

I follow the blue dots on the floor that guide me to the

reading room, a journey along hallways and stairwells that takes me deep into the basement of the library, where the reading room holding Juslenius's precious text awaits.

But first, a bit James Bond–style, I have to swipe my card under the digital reader and enter my password to open the gate that allows me access to the room where the treasured tome awaits.

Once through, I see his book from so long ago lying on a reserved table.

Each page of the leather-bound book, which is in surprisingly good shape given its age—more than 275 years old—is like a work of art, harking back to a time when the printed page ruled and hand-set typography was an art.

It is here in the reading room that I tap into a kind of bibliotherapy sisu, with a love for books, knowledge, the printed word, and the journeys that they take us on.

I also feel a sense of victory on another level. While a library visit may seem like a minor event, a little less than a year ago it would have seemed impossible.

As I turn the pages, there under the *S* on the slightly yellowed page, there it is, the word *sisucunda*, which at the time referred to a place in the human body where emotions could be felt. It's written in the eloquent cursive script of the time.

In this moment, I feel as though I've come full circle and

returned to one of the very sources of sisu: the place where the concept was first recorded.

This is the bookish version of an icy dip into the sea—a reminder that resilience in the face of life's challenges is an enduring and essential resource within us all. And even the issues, big or small, that may have initially seemed insurmountable can be tackled and solved with the right sisu approach.

AFTERWORD

THE COVID-19 PANDEMIC that started in 2020 took its toll on people around the world in so many ways and with so many losses. Human lives were lost and many people and businesses also suffered greatly.

Sadly, after this book was written both the Brooklyn Cafe and Restaurant Loop, each of which had been operating for many years, announced that they would be closing, in part owing to the losses incurred as a result of the pandemic.

Happily, the Brooklyn Cafe transferred some of its operations to its Brooklyn Baking Co., a bakery down the street from where their café once was.

A GLOSSARY OF FINNISH
WORDS RELATING TO SISU

AURINKO—Sun.

AVANTO—A hole carved into the ice, intended for a bracing dip.

AVANTOUINTI—Ice swimming, also known as winter swimming, is practiced during the cold months by taking a dip in the sea or a lake through a hole carved in the ice. A dip of just thirty seconds to a minute has many well-being benefits, including setting off the happy hormones, which leaves swimmers with a post-dip feeling of euphoria. *Avantouinti* is one of the key practices linked to happiness in Finland.

AVOIMUUS—Openness. Being open gives you the sisu superpower of being able to embrace new ideas and ways of thinking and living.

EKOTEKO—An environmentally friendly or sustainable action.

HALAUS—Hug.

HÄN—Gender-neutral pronoun for *he* or *she*. In the Finnish language, there is no *he* or *she*.

HENKIREIKÄ—Lifeline, though literally translated *henki* is "soul" and *reikä* is "hole."

HIIHTÄÄ—To ski.

HILJAISUUS—Silence.

HYMY—A smile.

HYÖTYLIIKUNTA—Functional or beneficial exercise that comes from an activity such as walking or cycling to work, housecleaning, or raking leaves.

JÄÄ—Ice.

JÄÄTELÖ—Ice cream. Finland consumes more ice cream per capita than any other European country.

JÄRVI—Lake.

JUHANNUS—Midsummer, the night in June when the sun doesn't set in many parts of Finland. People often go to countryside cottages and celebrate.

KAHVI—Coffee. Per capita, Finland is one of the top coffee-drinking countries in the world.

KEHO—Body.

KESTÄVÄ, KEHITYS—Sustainable development.

KIERRÄTETTY—Recycled.

KIRPPUTORI—Flea market. The place to stock up on secondhand clothing and household items or score some timeless Finnish design classics.

KOIVU—Birch, the national tree of Finland, also known as the "tree of life."

KOULUTUS—Education. Compulsory from age seven (grade one) to eighteen, and free of charge.

KUNNIOTTAA—Respect.

LÄPINÄKYVYS—Transparency.

LÖYLY—The steam that rises in the sauna when water is poured over the hot rocks on the stove.

LUMI—Snow.

LUONTO—Nature.

LUOTTAMUS—Trust.

MARJA—Berry.

ME—Pronounced "me." Means we.

MERI—Sea.

METSÄ—Forest, the place to be in Finland, 70 percent of which is covered by trees.

MIELI—Mind.

MÖKKI—Cottage.

NÖYRÄ—Humble.

ONNELLISUUS—Happiness.

OPPIA—To learn.

PAKKANEN—Frost.

POLKUPYÖRÄ—Bicycle.

PUU—Tree.

RAKKAUS—Love.

RÄNTÄ—Sleet.

RAUHA—Peace.

REHELLISYYS—Honesty.

ROHKEUS—Courage.

RUOKA—Food.

SADE—Rain.

SAUNA—The quintessential Finnish steam bath. It's estimated that there are 3.3 million saunas in Finland, which has a population of 5.5 million people. The best sauna experience is one by a sea or a lake, for a post-steam swim.

SIENI—Mushroom.

SISU—A unique form of fortitude and courage in the face of challenges, big and small.

SISUKAS—To have sisu.

SYDÄN—Heart.

SYDÄNYSTÄVÄ—A true friend.

TALVIPYÖRÄILY—Winter cycling.

TASA-ARVO—Equality.

TERVETULOA!—Welcome!

TIETO—Information.

TOIVO—Hope; also a male first name.

TUKI—Support.

VAHVA—Strong.

VALO—Light.

VESI—Water.

VOIMA—Power, strength.

VOIMAVARAT—Resources, reserves of strength.

YHDESSÄ—Together.

YSTÄVÄ—Friend.

ACKNOWLEDGMENTS

I'M FULL OF gratitude to so many people, for this book would not exist without its numerous cheerleaders. When I have gone through extremely rough patches, there have been so many kind souls who have continued to support and believe in me.

They include: my son, Felix, who inspires me every day with his loveliness, laughter, and wisdom; my parents, Satu and Tapio, who instilled in me a love of literature and a curiosity about the world and have supported me through thick and thin; my dear friends, including (in alphabetical order so as not to discriminate): Connie, Elina, Heli, Henrik, Marja, Max, Peppi, Riikka, Riina (who has also supported me by buying about a dozen or more of my books over the years), Sam, Tiina, and Veikko; and Harpal, who takes good care of my son when I'm working or away.

Without my agent, Elina Ahlbäck, whose patience and encouragement have been incomparable, and her team including Toomas Aasmäe, Ebba Erolin, Julia Kellums, and Rhea Lyons in New York, there would be no book. The same goes for my brilliant editor Marian Lizzi, at TarcherPerigee/Penguin Random House US in New York, and Hiroshi Shimizu, with Japanese publisher Hojosha, who both took on this book even before it was written, helping to make it happen, as did a generous writing grant from JOKES, the Finnish Foundation for the Promotion of Journalistic Culture.

I also owe massive thanks to all of my absolutely lovely interviewees and fact-checkers, for without their expertise and their stories, there would be little text here. A huge thank-you to Emilia Elisabet Lahti, the goddess of sisu, for your ongoing inspiration; Visit Peace's Essi Nousu; Brooklyn Cafe's Sharron and Brenda Todd; fellow journalist and dear friend Tiina Torppa, my source for sussing out all things Finnish; Licence to Fail's Tomi Kaukinen (and Shelly Nyqvist, who introduced me to Tomi's work); resiliency coach Ulrika Björkstam; Forestmind founder Sirpa Arvonen; Solar Foods cofounders Pasi Vainikka and JP Pitkänen; Micropolis's Johanna Jakku-Hiivala and her friend Heidi Takolo; Ii's mayor, Ari Alatossava; Ii's climate heroes Helmi, Nea, and Hanna; psychologist and bullying expert Vesa Nevalainen; Y-Foundation's Johanna Lassy; sustainable development expert Johanna Kohvakka; sister of sisu and education expert Jenni Kallio; University of Helsinki's Ilmari Määttänen; VTT's Johanna Närvänen; professor and environmental physiologist Mike Tipton; City of Helsinki cycling coordinator Oskari Kaupinmäki; video and performance artist Roberta Lima; biologist and wild food adviser Anna Nyman; Katja Liuksiala from Lapinlahden Lähde; Finnish language expert Ville Eloranta; sister of sisu and nurse Kaija Suni; the teachers at my son's school; VEEN Waters for permission to reuse part of an article I'd written for them on eco-anxiety; and Riikka Toivanen, who first introduced me to winter swimming several years ago.

My first readers, Tiina Torppa, Peppi Sala, Riina Tamm, Satu Pantzar, and Tapio Pantzar, provided invaluable feedback.

Thanks also to my self-appointed Czech father Jan Maruška, who invited me to and organized a visit to the Prague Book Fair a few years ago and made a huge impact on me and encouraged me to continue writing.

FILI, the Finnish Literature Exchange, which invited me to the Frankfurt Book Fair in 2019 to represent Finland, bestowed a huge honor on me. And this led to a conversation on the trade floor with the fabulous literary consultant and publicist Kimberly Burns, of New York, which helped to spur this book on. Kimberly said, "You know, you should write a book called *Daily Sisu*." I felt a tingle, as my agent and I already had a proposal by that name in the works; it was one of those big moments that restore your faith in what you're doing.

I also owe a big thank-you to my readers from around the world, who often seem to have an uncanny knack for reaching out and sending a supportive message or telling me that my writing has helped them or even been life-changing just when I feel as though I'm running low on sisu.

And a thank-you goes to my fellow year-round outdoor swimmers, who, with every swim, manage to make every day just a little bit brighter.

BIBLIOGRAPHY AND
REFERENCES

Aalto, Maija (January 11, 2021). Näin toimivat vakavan koulukiusaamisen katkaisemisen erikoisjoukot Helsingissä: "Me olemme kaikkien lasten puolella." *Helsingin Sanomat.*

Abend, Lisa (2020). Finland's Sanna Marin, the world's youngest female head of government, wants equality, not celebrity. *Time.*

Arvonen, Sirpa (2016). *Metsämieli.* Helsinki: Metsäkustannus.

Aurelius, Marcus (2004). *Meditations.* London: Penguin Books.

Benke, Erika (Producer) (2019, April 27). Finland's new generation of climate heroes. BBC.

Carrington, Damian (2020, October 14). Greener play areas boost children's immune systems, research finds. *Guardian.*

City of Helsinki Urban Environment Publications 2020:32 (2020). *Bicycle action plan 2020–2025.* Helsinki.

Donadio, Rachel (2020, April 1). How a millennial prime minister is leading Finland through crisis. *Vogue.*

Duxbury, Charlie (2019, July 18). To help the homeless, close a shelter. Politico.

Gash, Juliette (2020, January 24). How Finland solved its homelessness problem. RTE.

Glenny, Helen (2020, July 24). Cold water swimming: Why an icy dip is good for your mental and physical health. *BBC Science Focus*.

Gross, Jenny, and Johanna Lemola (2021, April 20). What makes a happy country? *New York Times*.

Helliwell, John F., Richard Layard, Jeffrey D. Sachs, and Jan-Emmanuel De Neve (eds.) (2020). *World happiness report 2020*. New York: Sustainable Development Solutions Network.

Helliwell, John F., Richard Layard, Jeffrey D. Sachs, and Jan-Emmanuel De Neve (eds.) (2021). *World happiness report 2021*. New York: Sustainable Development Solutions Network.

Henley, Jon (2019, December 9). Finland anoints Sanna Marin, 34, as world's youngest serving prime minister. *Guardian*.

Henley, Jon (2020, May 7). Finnish basic income pilot improved wellbeing, study finds. *Guardian*.

Henley, Jon (2020, January 29). How Finland starts its fight against fake news in primary schools. *Guardian*.

Henley, Jon (2019, June 3). "It's a miracle": Helsinki's radical solution to homelessness. *Guardian*.

Henley, Jon, Philip Oltermann, Sam Jones, and Angela Giuffrida (2021, April 23). "Let children play": The educational message from across Europe. *Guardian*.

Johnson, Sarah (2019, June 26). Virtual visits: How Finland is coping with an ageing population. *Guardian*.

Kale, Sirin (2020, October 16). "In every position I've ever been in, my gender has always been the starting point": Sanna Marin opens up about sexism in politics. *Vogue*.

Kallio, Jenni (2016). *Opettamisen vallankumous: Opettajasta elinikäisen oppimisen valmentajaksi*. Helsinki: Tietosanoma.

Kalm, Merja, and Mira Mallius (2020). *Hyvä tyyppi: Supervoimien Käsikirja*. Helsinki: Lasten Keskus.

Kaski, Satu, and Vesa Nevalainen (2015). *Ikävät ihmiset: Kuinka selviytyä hankalien tyyppien kanssa*. Helsinki: Kirjapaja.

Kaski, Satu, and Vesa Nevalainen (2013). *Jo riittää: Irti Kiusaamisesta ja kiusaajista*. Helsinki: Kirjapaja.

Kaski, Satu, and Vesa Nevalainen (2013). *Oy Ihminen Ab: Elämisen Jalo Taito*. Helsinki: Kirjapaja.

Kaski, Satu, and Vesa Nevalainen (2011). *Pessimisti ei pety: Eli miksi elämässä ei aina kannata odottaa liikoja.* Helsinki: Kirjapaja.

Konnikova, Maria (2016, February 11). How people learn to become resilient. *New Yorker.*

Lahti, Emilia (2019). Embodied fortitude: An introduction to the Finnish construct of sisu. *International Journal of Wellbeing* 9(1).

Lomas, Tim (2018). *Translating happiness: A cross-cultural lexicon of well-being.* Cambridge, MA: The MIT Press.

Lomas, Tim (2018, March 7). What Finnish can teach us about resilience. *Psychology Today.*

Lunt, Heather C., Martin J. Barwood, Jo Corbett, and Michael J. Tipton (2010). "Cross-adaptation": Habituation to short repeated cold-water immersions affects the response to acute hypoxia in humans. *Journal of Physiology,* 588(18), 3605–3613.

Määttänen, Ilmari; Henttonen, Pentti; Plomp, Johan; Honka, Anita; Lahti, Emilia; and Närväinen Johanna, (February 2020) Oral presentation on comprehensive new study on Finnish sisu at University of Helsinki.

Mahboob, Tahiat (2020, January 24). Housing is a human right: How Finland is eradicating homelessness. *Sunday Magazine.* CBC.

Marc, Jenny, and Mark Tutton (2020, January 20). This company says it's making food from "thin air" . . . plus a dash of water and clean energy. CNN.

Maté, Gabor (2019). *When the body says no: Exploring the stress-disease connection* (2nd ed.). London: Vermilion.

Nagoski, Emily, and Amelia Nagoski (2020). *Burnout: Solve your stress cycle.* London: Vermillion.

Närväinen, Johanna (2020, February 12). Comprehensive new study on Finnish sisu looks at how grit affects the way Finns work. VTT Technical Research Centre of Finland.

Nichols, Wallace J. (2014). *Blue mind: How water makes you happier, more connected and better at what you do.* London: Abacus/Little Brown UK.

Obordo, Rachel (2019, December 10). "The country faces a bright future": Finnish readers on their new PM. *Guardian.*

People Fixing the World (2020, February 4). The miracle cure: Exercise. Podcast. BBC.

Pihkala, Panu (2019). *Climate anxiety*. Helsinki: MIELI Mental Health Finland.

Rowlatt, Justin (2020, October 19). Could cold water hold a clue to a dementia cure? BBC.

Siivonen, Riku (2018, October 30). Tämän vuoksi jokaisen suomalaisen pitäisi viettää kymmenen viikkoa mielisairaalassa. Yle.

Tipton, M. J., N. Collier, H. Massey, J. Corbett, and M. Harper (2017). Cold water immersion: Kill or cure? *Experimental Physiology,* 102(11), 1335–1355.

Tomasulo, Dan (2020). *Learned hopefulness: The power of positivity to overcome depression*. Oakland, CA: New Harbinger.

Townsend, Dorn (2020, October 14). Helsinki makes sustainability a guiding principle for development. *New York Times.*

Van der Kolk, Bessel (2014). *The body keeps the score: Mind, brain and body in the transformation of trauma*. New York: Penguin Random House.

Vasama, Tanja (2021, January 18). Ruskea rasva voi suojata sairauksilta, ja erityisen paljon se hyödyttää ylipainoisia—Näillä keinoilla ruskeaa rasvaa voi aktivoida. *Helsingin Sanomat.*

Walker, Peter (2020, February 8). Why Finland leads the field when it comes to winter cycling. *Guardian.*

Walker, Peter (2020, February 7). Winter wheelies: Finland blazes trail in keeping citizens cycling and healthy. *Guardian.*

Y-Foundation (2017). *A home of your own: Housing First and ending home-lessness in Finland*. Keuruu, Finland: Otava.

The following websites also provided invaluable background information:

Arctic Flavours Association: www.arktisetaromit.fi
BBC: www.bbc.co.uk
Business Finland: www.businessfinland.fi
Finnish Forest Association: www.forest.fi
Finnish mental health hub: mielenterveystalo.fi
The Guardian: www.theguardian.com

Helsingin Sanomat: www.hs.fi
Lapinlahden Lähde: Lapinlahdenlahde.fi
The Martha Organization: Martat.fi
MIELI Mental Health Finland: www.mieli.fi
Municipality of Ii: www.ii.fi
Sisu researcher Emilia Lahti's website: emilialahti.com
Statistics Finland: www.stat.fi
Suomen Latu, The Outdoor Association of Finland: www.suomenlatu.fi
UKK Institute: www.ukkinstituutti.fi/en
VTT Technical Research Centre of Finland: www.vttresearch.com
Y-Foundation: https://ysaatio.fi/en
Yle, the Finnish Broadcasting Company: yle.fi

Quoted material was printed with the kind permission of the authors.
And the Helsinki public library system (helmet.fi) was an indispensable source of books for research, as I was able to borrow most of the titles I needed.

ABOUT THE AUTHOR

KATJA PANTZAR is a Helsinki-based writer, editor, and journalist. Raised in Canada with stints in New Zealand and the UK, she swims in the Baltic Sea almost every day year-round. Her first well-being book, *The Finnish Way*, was translated into twenty-two different languages around the world.